ALASKA'S FISH

A GUIDE TO SELECTED SPECIES

ROBERT H. ARMSTRONG

D0107225

ALASKA NORTHWEST BOOKS™
Anchorage • Seattle • Portland

This book is dedicated to the memory of those who have lost their lives while studying, managing, and protecting Alaska's fish. At the end of my study on Dolly Varden, I wrote: "Our emotions throughout this study ranged to the extremes. We were euphoric when our research plans worked and when we discovered something that had not been known before. We were horrified when a co-worker was mauled by a brown bear, and devastated when two colleagues working in the Arctic disappeared without a trace."

Acknowledgments

Many people helped me by providing information through interviews, sending publications, or editing the manuscript and selected articles. I specially thank Ellen Campbell, Richard Carlson, Jack Helle, Mike Mills, June Sage, Herman Savikko, Art Schmidt, John Schoen, Mark Schwan, Michelle Sydeman, Ed Weiss, and Bruce Wing.

Library of Congress Cataloging-in-Publication Data
Armstrong, Robert H., 1936-
    Alaska's fish: a guide to selected species / by Robert H. Armstrong.
        p. cm.
    Includes bibliographical references (p. 88) and index.
    ISBN 0-88240-472-5
    1. Fishes—Alaska. I. Title.
QL628.A4A77 1996
597.09798—dc20   95-47350
                                                                       CIP

Originating Editor: Marlene Blessing
Managing Editor: Ellen Harkins Wheat
Editor: Andrea Jarvela
Designer: Constance Bollen
Illustrations: Richard Carstensen
Map: Steve Podry, Vikki Leib

PHOTOS. Alaska Department of Fish and Game: 28,32; ANIMALS/ANIMALS, Robert Maier: 36, Oxford Scientific Films: 64, Doug Wechsler: 46, 52, 70, 74; Robert Armstrong: 12, 16, 24, 42, 48, 82; Richard Carlson: 6, 56; Daniel W. Gotshall: 20, 50-51, 54, 66, 68, 80; John Hyde: 10-11, 30; Mark Kelley: 22, 38; PHOTO RESEARCHERS, Berthoule: 34, Berthoule-Scott: 14, 40, Treat Davidson: 18, Tom McHugh: 26, 60; Rick Rosenthal: 44, 58, 62, 78; Ray Troll: 8; Doug Wechsler: 72, 76.

Front cover: *Kokanee*, Daniel W. Gotshall; Back cover: *Turbot*, Tom McHugh; End papers: *Salmon scales*, John Hyde; page 3: *Red Irish Lord*, Daniel W. Gotshall; page 5: *Lingcod*, Daniel W. Gotshall.

Alaska Northwest Books™
An imprint of Graphic Arts Center Publishing Company
Editorial office: 2208 NW Market Street, Suite 300, Seattle, WA 98107
Catalog and order dept.: P.O. Box 10306, Portland, OR 97210
Telephone: 1-800-452-3032

Printed on acid- and elemental-chlorine-free recycled paper in the United States of America

CONTENTS

Discovering Alaska's Fish • 6

DISCOVERING ALASKA'S FISH

My interest in Alaska's fish began in the early 1960s, when two of my colleagues and I were dropped off in a remote bay on Baranof Island in Southeast Alaska. We built a fish weir, a research station, and living quarters there, and later in the wilds of Admiralty Island. We discovered aspects of fish behavior and life histories within waters as wild and pristine as they had ever been. It was an exciting and rewarding time.

This book features many of the biological and behavioral insights biologists have gained about Alaska's fish. I have included fish that we catch in our commercial, subsistence, and sport fisheries; species that are important food for other fish and birds; and a few just plain weird ones. For each species, you'll find a photo, illustration, and brief essay that discusses such factors as unique physical features, habits, adaptation to Alaska's waters, and its role in Native culture. A fact box gives information on identification, life history, habitat, and range.

Alaska's fish, especially spawning salmon, are easily observed along streams, rivers, and coasts. Their behavior, as well as that of birds and mammals that feed on them, can be fascinating to watch. At the end of this book are a list of easily accessed sites and hints on how to watch fish and what to look for.

ALASKA, A SPECIAL PLACE FOR FISH

Alaska's fresh and salt waters support billions of fish that represent about 436 species: 52 freshwater or anadromous species and 384 saltwater species. Alaska has millions of freshwater lakes, ponds, rivers, and streams. Most are inhabited by fish for at least part of the year. The Alaska Department of Fish and Game has identified about 13,000 streams and 2,000 lakes as containing anadromous fish; many more are thought to exist. One such lake—Iliamna, with a surface area of 1,000 square miles—is the largest sockeye salmon–producing lake in the world. Several major rivers that originate in Canada cross the state before entering the ocean. Of these, the Yukon is the largest: it drains about 330,000 square miles and flows 2,300 miles from British Columbia to the Bering Sea.

Alaska's 170 to 233 million acres of wetlands—roughly 70 percent of the nation's total—are essential to the state's fish. Many species live directly in or near wetland habitat, but even wetlands inaccessible to fish benefit them. They provide nutrients and food to waters where fish live, buffer floods, and filter out pollutants.

Alaska's 34,000-mile-long shoreline—approximately 38 percent of the total length of the U.S. coast—forms myriad fjords, channels, lagoons, and bays. Two oceans—the North Pacific and Arctic—and three seas—the Bering, Chukchi, and Beaufort—border the state. Fish migrate from all northwestern states, Canada, Japan, and Russia to feed in these food-rich waters. Alaska also has almost 21 million acres of estuarine habitat—slightly more than exists for all the rest of the United States. These estuaries are important nursery grounds for salmon and many marine fish. They, in conjunction with our fresh waters, also contribute essential nutrients to the food chain of our oceans.

To live in Alaska's waters, many fish have developed special behavioral and physiological mechanisms. In fresh water, this usually means avoiding being frozen in ice during winter. Most do this by migrating to lakes, deeper portions of rivers, and warmer spring-fed areas. Our freshwater fish adapt to Alaska's short growing season and cold waters by living longer, growing

◀ *The decorated warbonnet is a prickleback found in rocky areas among seaweed from Southeast Alaska to the Bering Sea.*

more slowly, and maturing at an older age than their southern counterparts.

Fish living in the Arctic Ocean have a special problem: in winter, the temperature of the sea drops to a point at which most fish would freeze and die. Some, such as Dolly Varden, avoid freezing by migrating into rivers and living in spring areas. Others, such as salmon, migrate into warmer seas. Most marine fish, however, have evolved anti-freeze proteins in their blood plasma. This prevents them from freezing and allows them to remain in the supercooled winter environment.

Ketchikan artist Ray Troll gives us an idea of what it is like to be a fish in his painting *There is no free lunch*. Big fish eat little fish. Some species, like the Pacific sand lance, are essential food for fish that people eat, such as salmon. Even those species that are at the top of the food chain, such as sharks, provide important food for other fish when they die. Many species living deep in the ocean depend on the carcasses of dead fish for food. Most fish species produce tremendous numbers—some in the millions—of eggs and young each year that are essential food for other fish and sometimes even for themselves.

Alaska's fish are also essential to the health and survival of birds and mammals. Enormous numbers of seabirds that nest here—about 50 million each year—feed primarily on fish. In addition, the food-rich waters of the North Pacific Ocean and Bering Sea attract between 35 and 85 million seabirds that nest in other countries but migrate to Alaska to feed. Fish are also the mainstay of loons, mergansers, cormorants, great blue herons, belted kingfishers, bald eagles, seals, Steller sea lions, whales, river otters, mink, and many bears. The carcasses of spawned-out salmon contribute important nutrients to watersheds, which benefit plants, insects, and other animals that feed on them.

Alaska's commercial fisheries contribute significantly to the nation's food supply, generating billions of dollars in revenue.

Most Native villages in Alaska depend on fish for subsistence—recent annual salmon subsistence harvests have approached 900,000 fish statewide. The sport fishery in Alaska has also grown—to over 400,000 anglers harvesting about 3 million fish per year and catching and releasing another 3 million.

Overall, our government agencies and management and regulatory groups have done a good job managing and protecting Alaska's fish. Thanks to these agencies, environmental organizations, and concerned citizens, Alaska has 130 million acres of national wildlife refuges and parklands that help protect fish habitat. Many of our fish stocks have remained strong while others elsewhere have declined. In Alaska, commercial salmon harvests and escapements have been at all-time highs in recent years and the overall abundance of groundfish and Pacific herring in the Gulf of Alaska has been stable or rising.

Alaska's fish do have problems, however, and face an uncertain future as our human population and development increase. The numbers of freshwater fish are declining in many areas of the state because of increasing pressure from anglers. Fish are shrinking in size throughout the North Pacific Ocean—perhaps due to competition for food by the enormous numbers of salmon released from hatcheries in North America, Japan, and Russia or to climatic and oceanographic changes. Damage to fish habitat has occurred throughout Alaska—especially near cities and in areas of logging, mining, and oil development. Some politicians are trying—with some success—to change environmental laws and open up protected lands to make it easier to "develop" Alaska. If this happens, Alaska's fish will suffer. One need only look at what has happened to fish elsewhere to realize that it could also happen here.

External Features of Fish

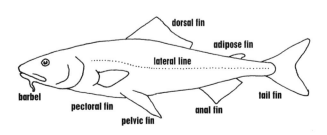

FRESHWATER AND ANADROMOUS FISH

Pink salmon schooling in Anan Creek near Wrangell in Southeast Alaska.

ALASKA BLACKFISH

The Alaska blackfish is a sluggish fish that cruises among the weeds along a river or lake bottom looking for a meal. It usually swims slowly, propelled by large paddle-like pectoral fins. But when it spots prey, it acts quickly, snatching the victim with a quick lunge.

This little fish is uniquely equipped to survive drought because it can breath air. Its esophagus has evolved to absorb gas, so it can exist off oxygen from the atmosphere. This adaptation allows it to live in small stagnant tundra or muskeg pools that lose oxygen in summer. It can even survive long dry periods in moist tundra mosses until rain refills the swamps and ponds.

Before winter freezes Alaska's small lakes and rivers, the blackfish migrates into larger lakes. Yet even these lakes may become low in oxygen during winter. Under these conditions, the blackfish seeks open areas in the ice, where it can surface and gulp air. Alaska Natives search for breaks in the ice where blackfish come to breathe or cut a hole to attract them. The fish concentrate near these holes in large numbers, making them easy to capture.

Eskimos use a simple, funnel-shaped trap made from strips of tamarack, spruce, or small-mesh wire cloth to trap the congregated fish. One Eskimo name for blackfish is *oonyeeyh*, which means "to sustain life."

Since the best blackfish lakes are those with the most associated otter and mink sign, they appear to help sustain the life of other mammals as well.

Because the blackfish can breathe atmospheric oxygen, it is very hardy, surviving under conditions that can kill other species. Natives who regularly harvest blackfish claim they are always abundant. Some people keep them alive in tubs of water, retrieving them as needed. Others simply cover a bunch of these fish in a snow pile; the blackfish mill about in a squirming mass under the snow, creating a little pond of melted water in the middle where they can stay alive for many days. Such tales have generated a myth that this fish can withstand being completely frozen, but biologists have found this to be untrue.

ALASKA BLACKFISH

▶ *It's a Fact:* This fish is a major prey item for northern pike and is also eaten by burbot, inconnu, river otters, mink, and loons.

Identification: Large paddle-like pectoral fins and tail, tiny pelvic fins with 2 to 3 rays, backward placement of dorsal and anal fins, and broad flat heads. Dark green or brownish on upper sides, pale belly, and irregular black blotchy areas on back and sides. Mature males have a reddish fringe along dorsal, tail, and anal fins. Maximum length 8 to 13 inches.

Spawning: May to August. Females may release only a portion of their 40 to 300 eggs at a time. Eggs adhere to vegetation and hatch into tiny young in about 9 days.

Life Span: About 4 years in Interior Alaska; up to 8 years in Bristol Bay.

Food: Aquatic insects and smaller fish. Larger blackfish eat smaller blackfish and northern pike.

Habitat and Range: Densely vegetated areas of lowland swamps, ponds, lakes, and rivers in Interior and Western Alaska. Found only in Alaska and eastern Siberia. Introduced into the Anchorage area.

ARCTIC CHAR

I was introduced to the culinary attributes of arctic char at a banquet during the first International Symposium on Arctic Char in Winnipeg, Manitoba, in 1981. Diners were served a delicate, flaky char fillet. It was delicious! Europeans and Eskimos knew about this tasty fish long before I did. As early as the eighteenth century, char pies—weighing up to 62 pounds each—were popular in England. This fish was a crucial subsistence food for Eskimos, especially in Canada, where they harvested char with stone weirs and spears made from musk ox horn and polar bear bone.

In Alaska, this fish is a lake resident. The arctic char that we think we see migrating to sea is another char species, the Dolly Varden, which looks very similar. Dolly Varden are so similar to char that biologists must count projections on their gills (called gill rakers) and projections on their intestine (called pyloric caeca) in order to determine which species is which. And even these characteristics overlap, causing some taxonomists to consider arctic char and Dolly Varden as the same species.

At one time, the char was believed to be a threat to salmon runs in Bristol Bay. Arctic char concentrating in rivers of the Wood River lakes feed heavily on migrating young sockeye salmon smolts. To protect the salmon run, biologists once captured and held char in net pens until the salmon smolts had safely passed. Temporarily holding them was considered better than killing them because char play another important role in the ecosystem: they feed on sticklebacks, which compete with sockeye young for food, and they eat freshwater snails that harbor a parasite that infects the eyes of salmon smolts. Also, arctic char are highly prized by anglers as a sport fish and by Natives as a subsistence food.

The arctic char is truly a fish of the Arctic. Its circumpolar range extends throughout northern Russia, Norway, Iceland, Greenland, Canada, and Alaska. It mostly inhabits bodies of fresh water formed on land that has emerged only recently—in geologic time—from beneath the Pleistocene ice cap or has been uplifted from beneath the sea.

ARCTIC CHAR

▶ *It's a Fact:* A Norwegian study of this fish discovered that it can distinguish other fish groups by smell. The char detects odors, called pheromones, in extremely minute amounts, which may help it find its home stream to spawn.

Identification: Nearly identical to Dolly Varden. Usually 23 to 32 rakers on first gill arch and 35 to 75 pyloric caeca. Silver overall to dark blue to dark green or brown on back and sides; silver or dull white on belly; pink to red spots on side; red, orange, or yellow on paired fins. Spawning males may be intense red all over. Distinguished from trout and salmon by the lack of black spots. Juveniles have 10 to 15 irregularly placed parr marks. Most 2 to 4 pounds, some to 11; to 30 pounds in Canada.

Spawning: September to November. Mature at age 6 to 8. Spawn annually after maturity in Western Alaska and in alternate years on the North Slope. Spawn over gravel shoals near stream mouths.

Life Span: Up to 13 years.

Food: Salmon smolts, sticklebacks, freshwater snails, and insects.

Habitat and Range: Lakes on Kodiak Island, Alaska Peninsula, Bristol and Kuskokwim Bay drainages, Brooks Range, and North Slope.

ARCTIC GRAYLING

The arctic grayling was once common throughout the northern part of the Lower 48 states. But habitat loss, pollution, competition from introduced species, and overfishing nearly eliminated this species from areas outside Alaska and Canada. This beautiful fish is now usually associated with the northern wilderness. Indeed, Alaska's clear, cold, unpolluted waters provide it with ideal habitat.

The arctic grayling has adapted to a wide variety of Alaska's waters because it spawns in spring and early summer and its eggs and larvae develop relatively fast. This early and rapid development enables the adults and young to spawn and feed in rivers and streams that will freeze in winter and are thus uninhabitable.

Adapting to different systems—or different parts of the same system—has resulted in complex migrations to overwintering, spawning, and feeding sites. Many streams in Alaska's Interior freeze solid or dry up in winter, especially the bog-fed ones. Hence, the grayling migrates out of these streams to overwinter in waters that don't freeze. These include large lakes and rivers, such as the Yukon, Kuskokwim, and Tanana in the Interior, and areas with extensive springs in the Arctic.

The distances that grayling migrate to reach overwintering sites vary considerably. Some spend all or part of their lives near their overwintering areas; others migrate up to 100 miles. Alaskan grayling may also migrate to streams where food is more abundant to feed or to streams where there is suitable habitat to spawn.

When spawning, the male grayling stakes out a territory in a riffle area and courts females as they swim into his turf. Spreading his huge dorsal fin, he moves sideways toward the female. She may reject several potential mates before choosing one. Her selected mate covers her back with his dorsal fin and, with the aid of his tail fin, presses the back end of her body into the gravel. This allows the eggs and sperm to be deposited just below the gravel surface, where they are better protected.

The egg develops rapidly, hatching within 8 to 18 days. The new hatchling—which has been described as "two eyeballs on a thread"—remains in the gravel for 3 or 4 days. As they emerge from the gravel, young grayling are nearly helpless and cannot swim against a current, so they form dense schools and move into still waters where their chances of survival are greater. They remain in these protected areas until late summer, when they become territorial and solitary and move into deeper waters with stronger currents.

ARCTIC GRAYLING

▶ *It's a Fact:* This fish can tolerate low dissolved oxygen levels and survive long winters under the ice— conditions that would kill many other fish.

Identification: Large dorsal fin, small mouth. Iridescent gray sides; dorsal fin has large, iridescent red or green spots; scattered black spots on sides. Young have narrow, vertical parr marks. State angling record is 4 pounds, 13 ounces. Largest come from Bristol Bay area.

Spawning: Mid-May to mid-June. Most reach maturity at age 4 to 8. Female lays from 1,700 to over 14,000 eggs.

Life Span: Average 7 years; maximum age to 22 years.

Food: Insects, salmon eggs and fry, sticklebacks, and occasionally water shrews.

Habitat and Range: Native in lakes, rivers, and streams throughout most of Alaska. Introduced into Southeast and Kodiak Island.

BURBOT

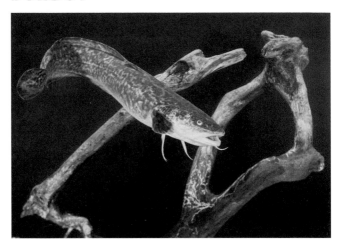

The burbot is the only member of the cod family in North America that lives exclusively in fresh water. With its large head and long tapered body, it is one of the strangest-looking freshwater fish in Alaska, but it is delicious. Fish biologists in Fairbanks once sponsored an annual fish fry where one could sample species from all over Alaska. The burbot, with its firm, white flesh and large—thus easily avoided—bones, was usually the most popular.

As a predator, the burbot is well equipped. It has a large mouth, strong jaw, and numerous small teeth that slant backward toward the throat. It also has a well-developed sense of smell and keen eyesight, enabling it to find prey in murky waters and in low light under the ice.

Studies have shown that when other fish in Alaska are the least active, the burbot becomes most active. For instance, it is most active when light conditions are the lowest—at night in summer and under the ice in winter. Also, its digestive enzymes, and hence activity, increase as the water temperature drops, the opposite of other freshwater fish. These differences make the burbot a very efficient predator.

Little is known about how the burbot spawns in Alaska. Studies in Russia indicate that in winter burbot move upstream under the ice and spawn late in the season. They have been observed milling together in a large writhing ball when releasing their eggs and sperm. The tiny egg contains an oil droplet, which helps it to float about in the current. Some eventually settle among the rocks in backwater areas. Hatching peaks in late April before the ice breakup. The young burbot is very tiny—about ⅛ inch—and drifts downstream with the current. After the yolk sac is absorbed—probably after the ice breakup—young burbot form schools and reside in sunny areas among the vegetation in marshes.

The burbot likes deep water. In lakes it may be found as deep as 700 feet. In rivers it frequents the deeper areas near rocky bluffs, in back eddies, and near the mouths of clear-water tributary streams. When spawning, burbot move into the shallower areas of rivers.

BURBOT

▶ *It's a Fact:* This fish's name is from the French word *bourbeter*, which means to "wallow in mud."

Identification: 2 dorsal fins; front one short with 8 to 16 fin rays, back one very long with 60 to 80 fin rays. One long, thin barbel (chin whisker). Large head with small eye and long, slender body. Mottled olive-black or brown skin with yellowish patches. State angling record is 24 pounds, 12 ounces. Maximum size to 74 pounds and 60 inches.

Spawning: February and March. Mature at age 6 or 7, at about 18 inches. Spawn under the ice. Large female burbot may lay up to 3 million eggs; average is about 1 million.

Life Span: Up to 24 years.

Food: Up to age 4 eats mostly insects and other invertebrates. Fish over age 5 eat other small fish, such as other burbot, slimy sculpin, lampreys, whitefishes, young salmon, and arctic grayling. Occasionally eat swimming voles, shrews, and bank swallows.

Habitat and Range: Large glacial rivers, such as the Yukon and Tanana, in Alaska's Interior; lakes and streams in Interior, Southcentral, and the Arctic.

CHINOOK SALMON

The chinook (king) is Alaska's state fish and very popular in the state's commercial, subsistence, and sport fisheries. The largest commercial harvests come from Southeast, the Yukon River, Bristol Bay, and the Kuskokwim River. The latter three areas support the largest subsistence fisheries for chinook in Alaska. Major sport fisheries are centered in Southeast and Cook Inlet.

Chinook are the largest and least abundant of the Pacific salmon species found in Alaska. Many chinook that feed and are caught in Southeast Alaska come from elsewhere. At one time, freshwater systems like the Columbia River had spawning runs of 1 to 2 million or more fish every year. Chinook from the Columbia River were once particularly abundant in Southeast Alaska, but these runs were severely reduced by a host of environmental problems. Most of the chinook that frequent Alaska's marine waters outside of Southeast Alaska, especially in the very northern part of the Pacific Ocean and Bering Sea, are of Alaskan origin.

The chinook salmon differs from other Pacific salmon in its variable flesh color, which may range from white to pink or red. In Southeast, up to 40 percent of some runs are white-fleshed, whereas in the rest of Alaska most chinook are red-fleshed. The chinook's flesh color may be due to a genetic disposition or to its feeding habits. One study showed that red- and white-fleshed chinook salmon had identical chemical compositions, except for certain pigments called carotenoids, which are responsible for the red coloration in fish. Still, most people think red-fleshed salmon look and taste better, hence they cost more.

Chinook spawn in relatively few rivers compared to most other species of Pacific salmon, probably because their spawning requirements are more exacting. For example, chinook, like other salmon, tend to spawn only in areas that have a good flow of subsurface water through the gravel. Since chinook salmon have larger eggs than other salmon, their eggs require more oxygen and sites that can support them are limited.

The young of many chinook that spawn in rivers outside of Alaska migrate to estuaries shortly after emerging from the gravel. In Alaska, however, young chinook live in streams for at least 1 year, 2 years in more northerly rivers, before migrating to sea. During this freshwater rearing period, the young reside in flowing waters, often near and among logjams.

CHINOOK SALMON

▶ *It's a Fact:* Like other salmon in Alaska, the chinook is semelparous, which means it dies after spawning once.

Identification: Small black spots on tail lobes. Black along base of teeth. At sea, bluish green on back; silver on sides and white on belly. At spawning, red to copper to almost black. Juvenile has 6 to 12 large parr marks on side. State angling record is 97 pounds, 4 ounces; one 126-pounder was caught commercially near Petersburg.

Spawning: July to September. Female deposits from 3,000 to 14,000 eggs.

Life Span: 1 to 2 years in fresh water, 3 to 5 years at sea; some live 8 years. Spawn at age 4 to 7.

Food: Young in fresh water eat insects. Adults and young in salt water eat invertebrates and fish.

Habitat and Range: From Southeast to Yukon River. The largest runs enter the Yukon, Kuskokwim, Nushagak, Susitna, Kenai, Copper, Alsek, Taku, and Stikine Rivers.

CHUM SALMON

The chum has the widest geographical distribution of all Pacific salmon: from Korea to the Siberian Arctic and from California to the Alaskan and Canadian Arctic. Biologists estimate that chum salmon has a greater biomass than any other Pacific salmon species—upwards of 50 percent of the annual biomass of all salmon and well over 1 million tons in some years.

The chum is also called dog salmon. Where this name comes from becomes evident on its spawning grounds. The male chum salmon develops the typical hooked snout of salmon, but in chum this snout and lower jaw contain very large canine teeth. At this time it can be a very formidable creature—I have seen a chum tear holes in a biologist's hip boots, perhaps not by accident.

Male chum salmon fight with each other over spawning females. These skirmishes occasionally erupt into fierce battles that feature open-mouthed attacks, bites, and body blocks. Since a large male has the greatest chance to obtain a mate, a smaller male positions himself downstream from a courting pair and attempts to sneak in and fertilize some of her eggs while the mated pair are busy spawning.

Over most of its range, including Alaska, some chum populations return early to the spawning streams and some return late. Early-run chum spawn in main stems of streams, and the late spawners seek out spring-fed areas. Spring-fed areas provide a more constant year-round water flow and temperature, hence the water is less likely to freeze as winter approaches and temperatures drop. In the Yukon River drainage, the later chum is larger and has a brighter appearance because it has the farthest to go—over 2,000 miles without food—and needs more fat reserves.

One exceptionally late run has become world famous. In the Chilkat River near Haines, upwellings of warm water keep portions of the river ice-free throughout the winter. Here, large numbers of chum salmon spawn in October and November and provide food for a phenomenal gathering of bald eagles, numbering up to 3,500 at a time. This concentration of chums and eagles has resulted in the establishment of the Chilkat Bald Eagle Preserve.

CHUM SALMON

▶ *It's a Fact:* Spawned-out adult chum salmon are major food for bears and bald eagles. The young fry in fresh water are important food for coho young, Dolly Varden, cutthroat and rainbow trout, sculpins, mergansers, and kingfishers.

Identification: Black specks on back; no black spots on back and tail; 18 to 28 short, stout gill rakers and rudiments on first gill arch. At sea, metallic greenish blue on top; silver below. At spawning, has vertical bars of green and purple, white-tipped anal and pelvic fins. Female has dark horizontal band along side. Juvenile has 6 to 14 narrow, short parr marks. State angling record is 32 pounds; most range from 7 to 18.

Spawning: June to January (most July to November).

Female deposits from 2,000 to 4,000 eggs.

Life Span: Spawn at age 3, 4, or 5. All die after spawning.

Food: Young in fresh water eat aquatic insects. At sea, eat small invertebrates, fish, and squid larvae.

Habitat and Range: All coastal and offshore waters of Alaska, limited numbers along Arctic coast. Spawns in coastal streams from intertidal to 2,000 miles inland (Yukon drainage).

COHO SALMON

Coho, or silver, salmon may be the most successful of all salmon species, even though fewer of them spawn in Alaska's fresh waters than most other salmon species. While there aren't as many of them, spawning coho and their young seem to be in almost every accessible body of fresh water within their range.

The coho's successful habitation of small coastal streams is related to its aggressiveness and determination to reach small headwater creeks and tributaries to spawn. The adult coho seems to overcome obstacles that stop other salmon in their upstream journey. It can leap vertically more than 6 feet. It also migrates during fall floods, when water levels are higher and most other species have ceased spawning.

A female digs a nest in gravel by turning on her side and slapping her tail on the gravel surface to create a suction effect, which lifts up gravel and sand. The female tests the depth of the nest by "probing" the depression with her tail and anal fin. Almost immediately after depositing her eggs, she covers them with gravel. This gives her a start on another nest, which she usually constructs just in front of the first one.

About 1 month after hatching, coho fry emerge from the gravel to feed and begin to disperse. Eventually, many fry establish their own territories and become more aggressive, the larger ones nipping at and chasing away the smaller ones. As the fry become more aggressive, the hapless young that cannot find or defend a territory are displaced downstream, where they are more vulnerable to predators or may be swept out to sea. At this early stage of development, many cannot yet tolerate salt water and die. Yet, aggressive territoriality is beneficial to the species, assuring adequate space and food, hence survival, for those that remain.

Coho salmon adults and their young provide an important year-round source of food for other creatures. Since coho usually spawn late in the year, the carcasses of spawned-out fish often become trapped and preserved in the winter ice. During the occasional mid- to late-winter thaws, the frozen carrion becomes accessible to hungry eagles, wolves, and other mammals. The coho young that live year-round in these streams provide a steady food supply for kingfishers, mink, and river otters.

COHO SALMON

▶ *It's a Fact:* Although most coho spend about 1 1/2 years at sea before they return to fresh water to spawn, some precocious males called jacks return to spawn after only 6 months, when they are about 12 inches long.

Identification: Black spots on back and upper lobe of tail, white at base of teeth. At sea, dark metallic back, silver sides and underneath. At spawning, male has green back and red on sides; female is bronze to reddish on sides. Juvenile has white on leading edge of dorsal and anal fin; all fins may be tinted orange. State angling record is 26 pounds; most range from 7 to 12.

Spawning: October and November, some into January. Females deposit 2,400 to 4,500 eggs.

Life Span: Up to 5 years; most spawn at age 2 or 3.

Food: Young eat insects and pink and chum fry. At sea, coho eat marine invertebrates, salmon fry, and small fish.

Habitat and Range: Coastal salt water from Southeast to Point Hope on Chukchi Sea. Streams and rivers of all sizes, lakes, and beaver ponds; over 1,200 miles up Yukon River.

CUTTHROAT TROUT

Throughout its range the cutthroat trout, like a canary in a mine, is a sensitive indicator of environmental change. This species was once found in abundance throughout the American West. Now, except for Yellowstone Lake and River in Yellowstone National Park and a few other protected areas, this fish has vanished in the Lower 48. Its demise was caused by habitat loss resulting from human changes to the environment and widespread introduction of nonnative races of rainbow and brook trout. Introduced rainbow trout hybridized with the cutthroat, and brook trout competed with it for habitat and food.

Alaska is blessed with pristine fish habitat. In addition, the Alaska Department of Fish and Game prohibits introduction of nonnative fish species. Thus many "pure" populations of cutthroat are found here. They may be sea-run (anadromous), spend their entire life in a lake-stream system, or reside only in streams.

The sea-run cutthroat is usually associated with lakes and a few of the larger, slow-moving rivers. Most of these anadromous populations are found south of Frederick Sound in Southeast Alaska. Each year, the fish go to sea in May and June and return to fresh water in September and October.

Throughout the cutthroat's range in Alaska, freshwater systems containing seagoing salmonids number in the thousands, but probably less than 100 of these systems contain significant numbers of sea-run cutthroat trout. A good run may contain about 3,000 fish; of these, only about 300 to 400 may be maturing females that will spawn the following spring. In addition, the fish are relatively slow growing, taking about 5 to 6 years to reach maturity at a length of 10 to 12 inches. These factors make our sea-run cutthroat trout very sensitive to overfishing.

Resident cutthroat trout are found in most landlocked lakes at the lower elevations in Southeast Alaska. In a few of these systems, you may find large, trophy-sized cutthroat trout of 3 to 8 pounds. In contrast, most sea-run cutthroat seldom exceed 1 to 2 pounds. Some resident lake cutthroat grow large because they prey heavily on small landlocked sockeye salmon, called kokanee, and they are longer-lived than sea-run individuals. Other resident cutthroat have evolved ways to live their entire lives in streams so small you can easily step over them. They adapt to small spaces by spawning at an early age and growing to only a few inches.

CUTTHROAT TROUT

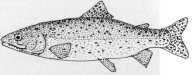

▶ *It's a Fact:* The name cutthroat refers to the distinctive red slash mark found under the fish's jaw.

Identification: Most have distinctive, vivid red to faint yellow slash mark under jaw; small teeth on floor of mouth between gill arches (both characteristics are missing in rainbow trout). Sea-run individuals uniformly silver with numerous black spots; lake residents golden yellow with numerous black spots. Young have about 10 oval parr marks. Anal fin has 8 to 12 rays. Resident lake cutthroat to 8 pounds, 24 inches; sea-run, 1 to 2 pounds, to 18 inches.

Spawning: Late April to early June. Spawn in small, headwater streams. From 750 to 1,200 eggs per pound of body weight.

Life Span: Lake residents to 19 years; stream residents to 5 years; sea-run to 10 years.

Food: Insects, invertebrates, and small fish.

Habitat and Range: Coastal areas from Prince William Sound south. Occurs in streams, lakes, bog ponds, and at sea.

DOLLY VARDEN

Fred DeCicco, Alaska fisheries biologist.

The sea-run Dolly Varden move around a lot in Alaska's southern coastal areas. Most spend the winter in lakes, migrate to the ocean in spring, enter other streams—sometimes several—and return to lakes in the fall. At maturity, a Dolly Varden leaves its lake wintering area and migrates directly to its home stream to spawn. A lake may harbor Dolly Varden originating from streams as far as 100 miles away. A Dolly Varden tagged in the Wulik River in northwest Alaska was recaptured 1,048 miles away in Siberia.

Overwintering in lakes may have several advantages for sea-run Dolly Varden. Because of ice cover there are few, if any, predators. In winter, fresh water in southern Alaska is several degrees cooler than seawater, so the fish needs fewer calories and less food. It may live longer because it does not need to burn energy to avoid predators, search for food, or swim against currents.

The sea-run Dolly Varden that live in Alaska's Arctic cope with harsher conditions. Most parts of arctic rivers freeze solid in winter and there are no suitable lakes with access to the sea for overwintering. Thus, spawning and overwintering waters are the major spring areas within the larger rivers, where the warmer spring waters prevent the river from freezing.

The sea-run Dolly Varden young live from 2 to 5 years in streams before going to sea. During this period the fish are very

28

territorial and fight among themselves. Each pool has a "despot" that defends the best feeding area. If another fish catches food in the despot's territory, it cruises around attacking any other young Dolly Varden it encounters.

In the 1920s and 1930s, a bounty was paid on Dolly Varden in Alaska because it was considered a serious predator on salmon eggs and young: more than 6 million were killed. Studies now show that the Dolly Varden may actually benefit salmon populations. It eats unburied salmon eggs, which eventually die and develop fungus that may infect healthy eggs and fry in the gravel. It feeds heavily on a freshwater snail that harbors a parasite that infects the eyes of coho and sockeye salmon young and eventually causes blindness. It also eats fish that compete for food with salmon young.

DOLLY VARDEN

▶ *It's a Fact:* This fish got its name because its coloring resembled the pink spotted dress and hat worn by Miss Dolly Varden in Charles Dickens's novel *Barnaby Rudge.*

Identification: Nearly identical to arctic char. Usually 14 to 21 rakers on first gill arch and 21 to 29 pyloric caeca. Sea-run before spawning are silvery with olive green to brown on top, red to orange spots on sides; freshwater residents are olive green to brown on back and sides with yellow, orange, or red spots. At spawning, male turns brilliant red or orange, with white front edge on lower fins; female similar but less brilliant. Juvenile has 8 to 12 parr marks. Most stream residents are 7 to 9 inches; sea-run 15 to 22 inches.

Spawning: September through October. Sea-run mature between 5 and 9 years, stream residents younger.

Life Span: To 18 years, most under 10.

Food: Insects, crustaceans, salmon eggs and young, and fish.

Habitat and Range: Lakes, large rivers, streams, and salt water. Throughout Alaska's coastal areas.

EULACHON

When eulachon spawn the banquet begins. Bald eagles, lined up wing to wing, feed along the riverbanks or wade right in, clusters of talons and beaks snatching at the swarming fish. Up to 1,500 eagles have been observed at one time feeding on spawning eulachon in the Stikine River in Southeast Alaska—the second-largest concentration of feeding eagles in North America.

Other animals join in the feast. Killer whales, beluga whales, seals, sea lions, bears, and gulls gather near the mouths of rivers and streams where huge schools of eulachon form as the spawning season approaches. When the water warms to just the right temperature the fish swim into the river, spawning in groups in the lower reaches.

The eulachon is a "broadcast" spawner. It spews eggs and sperm out into the water column, usually over a sandy bottom, rather than laying eggs directly on or into the substrate. Eulachon eggs have two membranes; the outer one ruptures quickly and turns inside out but remains attached to the inner membrane in one spot. The broken outer membrane contains a sticky substance that adheres the egg to sand grains or pebbles, where it incubates for 30 to 40 days until it hatches. The $1/4$-inch-long, transparent larval fish is quickly carried out to sea by the river current.

Eulachon is a traditional subsistence food for Alaska Natives. The harvested fish is rendered into oil, smoked or dried, or eaten fresh. The Natives use eulachon oil, the primary product, as a dietary supplement or food condiment. They also believe it has medicinal properties. The Tlingit believe that the eulachon (they call it *saak*) carries personality traits—happiness, contentment, and sensitivity—to its surroundings.

The Tlingit harvest eulachon with dip nets. They stand along the shore and sweep from side to side in long strokes, beginning upstream. They empty the fish into pits dug into the ground or into wooden bins and leave them to ferment for 7 to 10 days. Then they boil the fish in large steel vats for about 3 hours to render the oil, ladle it into clean buckets, allow it to settle, and pour it into jars for storage.

EULACHON

▶ *It's a Fact:* Eulachon, from the Chinook Indian word *ulakan*, means "candlefish." It got its name because when dried, you can insert a wick right into the fish and it will burn off the oil.

Identification: Only smelt species with circular grooves on gill covers; dorsal fin begins well behind where pelvic fin attaches. Spawning male has thickened ridge along side. Gray-brown at spawning, otherwise bluish silver. Smelts are small, slender fishes with a large mouth; they look similar to salmonids and have an adipose fin, but they lack the pelvic axillary process found in salmonids. To 10 inches.

Spawning: April and May. Mature at age 3 or 4. Females lay 17,000 to 60,000 eggs depending on size.

Life Span: Most die after spawning.

Food: Eulachon larvae eat phytoplankton, copepod eggs, copepods, mysids, ostracods, and larvae of various invertebrates. Juveniles and adults eat small shrimps and copepods.

Habitat and Range: Lower reaches of selected rivers (often glacier-fed) from Southeast to Cook Inlet when spawning; otherwise range throughout Pacific Ocean and into Bering Sea.

INCONNU or SHEEFISH

Ken Alt, Alaska sheefish biologist.

This is a fish of many appellations. Most Alaskans and biologists call it sheefish, but its official name is inconnu. Early French-Canadian explorers named it *poisson inconnu*, which means "unknown fish." It is also referred to as Eskimo tarpon because it resembles the tarpon, with its large mouth, silvery appearance, and habit of rising vertically out of the water and appearing to walk on its tail when hooked.

You may not be able to see a sheefish spawn, but you can hear it. In the evening, the female surfaces with a loud splash, then skitters across the water, expelling her eggs along the way. The males follow just behind and underneath her, releasing their sperm, usually without breaking the surface.

Sheefish eggs are slightly adhesive, and after they sink, settle in the gravel. The eggs incubate over the winter and begin hatching in mid-April. The tiny sheefish are swept downstream with the spring floods into the extensive deltas of the larger rivers.

The young sheefish begins feeding on plankton, then, as it grows, insects and eventually small fish. By the second year of its life it feeds mostly on fish. A voracious eater, the sheefish grows faster than any other arctic freshwater species—up to 16 inches at age 2 and 14 pounds by age 8.

Most Alaskan sheefish are estuarine anadromous. That is, they overwinter in estuaries or lower parts of rivers, then when the ice breaks up in May they migrate upstream to summer feeding areas. Mature sheefish eventually swim farther upstream—some travelling as far as 1,000 miles—to reach their spawning grounds.

Alaska's sheefish are thought to have originated in the rivers of Siberia, then spread to Alaska in brackish water. When this occurred is unknown, but sheefish fossils—dated to 60,000 years ago—have been found at Old Crow along the upper Yukon River.

One major use of sheefish in Alaska is as subsistence food for Alaska Natives and their dogs. In summer, sheefish are taken by seine and gill net as they move upstream. In winter, they were traditionally taken through holes in the ice by a jigging stick and hooks made of bear teeth and ivory, but modern rod and reel methods are now used.

SHEEFISH

▶ *It's a Fact:* Eskimos traditionally ate sheefish raw—but only after a slight preparation. First they buried the fish in leaf-lined pits and aged them for several weeks. They called this dish "stink fish." Its texture is described as cheese-like and its aroma as, well, stinky.

Identification: A whitefish, it can be distinguished from other members of this family by a large, wide mouth with lower jaw projecting beyond upper jaw. Mostly silvery with darker coloration on back, may exhibit a phosphorescent purple sheen when pulled from the water. State angling record is 53 pounds.

Spawning: Late September and early October. Female matures from age 7 to 11, male from age 5 to 9. Most females spawn every other year and release up to 400,000 eggs for a 50-pound female.

Life Span: Up to 21 years.

Food: Adults eat lampreys, whitefishes, northern pike, longnose suckers, young salmon, and occasionally other sheefish.

Habitat and Range: Found only in arctic and subarctic areas of Alaska, Canada, and Siberia. Inhabit larger, slower-moving river systems—Kuskokwim, Yukon, and Selawik-Kobuk.

LAKE TROUT

A lake trout is a rather fussy fish. It does not like warm water or light. Its rejection of light earns it the impressive scientific descriptor "negatively phototropic" and residence in the deepest parts of mountain lakes, especially during the summer. Its upper lethal temperature, 74°F, is one of the lowest for freshwater fish. As a result, as summer progresses and lakes become warmer, the trout descends into the depths and cooler water. In spring, before lakes warm up, and during summer twilight hours, the trout may swim near the surface or move inshore to feed.

Unlike its salmonid relatives, the lake trout spawns only at night (dusk to late evening), does not pair up, and does not construct a nest. Spawning may involve several males and females. Eggs and sperm are broadcast over rocks, where they settle into crevices. The male arrives on the spawning grounds before the female and rubs his snout, body, and tail over the substrate. Some biologists think the fish is cleaning algae and detritus off the rubble; others believe it is scent-marking the rocks with an odor that attracts females.

Alaska's mountain lakes, where the lake trout resides, are harsh, nutrient-poor environments, so it grows very slowly, matures late in life, and may not spawn every year. The adult is a solitary creature, and not very many lake trout live in each lake. These combined factors leave our lake trout populations very susceptible to over-harvest by anglers. Fortunately for the lake trout,

34

it is a "terminal predator," which means that the adult is seldom eaten by other fish. One exception occurred in the Great Lakes, where parasitic sea lamprey decimated lake trout stocks. The non-native lamprey entered the Great Lakes when the Welland Canal opened between Lake Ontario and Lake Erie in 1829.

The lake trout, like many other slow-growing northern fish, is difficult to age with its scales. The growth rings, much like those in a cut tree, are too close together. Biologists have found that its age can be determined more accurately by counting rings on its otoliths. These otoliths, located in the head, are calcified tissues used for equilibrium, balance, and hearing. Using otoliths, biologists aged a lake trout from the Northwest Territories in Canada at 62 years, the oldest determined so far.

LAKE TROUT

▶ *It's a Fact:* The lake trout is a member of the salmonid family, but it is not a trout. It belongs to the same genus as arctic char and Dolly Varden, hence it is really a char.

Identification: Deeply forked tail, absence of pink spots on sides. Color variable but generally silvery to dark gray with numerous, small, cream or yellow, irregular-shaped spots. Breeding male has dark stripe on side, lacks red or orange of Dolly Varden and arctic char. Juvenile has 7 to 12 narrow parr marks. State angling record is 47 pounds; world record is 102.

Spawning: September through November. Mature at age 7 or 8 in the Interior, 10 to 20 in Northern Alaska.

Females lay from 300 to 13,000 eggs.

Life Span: Most about 20 years; some over 50.

Food: Insects, mollusks, crustaceans, and rodents. Sculpins, least cisco, humpback whitefish, round whitefish, arctic grayling, northern pike, burbot, and other lake trout.

Habitat and Range: Mountain lakes of Brooks Range; arctic coastal plain; upper Tanana, Susitna, and Copper River drainages; and Kenai Peninsula.

▲▼▲▼▲▼▲▼▲▼▲▼▲▼▲▼▲▼▲▼▲▼▲▼▲▼▲▼▲▼▲▼▲▼▲▼▲▼▲ ▲▼▲▼

NORTHERN PIKE

The northern pike hunts its quarry like a cat after a mouse, stealthily approaching to within striking distance, then attacking with a sudden, explosive dart. Or it may simply lurk among the vegetation and pounce on its prey as it swims by. At the last second, the pike opens its mouth, sucking in its prey.

This fish is well equipped for its predatory lifestyle. Its camouflage colors conceal it among the aquatic vegetation. It has a long, flat, duckbill-like snout filled with sharp canine teeth on its jaws and smaller, well-developed teeth on the roof of its mouth and tongue. Like sharks' teeth, the pike's teeth are constantly replaced.

The pike is a voracious carnivore and will eat any living creature it can swallow—frogs, mice, muskrats, and even ducklings. Biologists in Canada estimate that these fish may eat about 1.5 million young waterfowl per year. But Alaska's ducklings only occasionally show up as pike food. Other pike are not so overlooked—this fish is very cannibalistic, and in some areas its own kind are the most frequently eaten item.

In late fall and early winter, as the pike's favorite hunting grounds—the shallow vegetated areas—dry up or become icebound, it moves to the deeper parts of lakes and rivers for the winter. It moves back to quiet or slow-moving shallows to spawn soon after the ice recedes in the spring. There, the female broadcasts her eggs, which adhere to vegetation, rocks, or other debris.

The egg incubates for up to 30 days. Then it hatches into a tiny, 1/4-inch-long, mouthless prolarva that lives off its yolk sac for about 15 to 20 days. Now about 1/2 inch long, the tiny fish's mouth has developed, and it begins feeding on small invertebrates.

This fish is delicious to eat; its meat is white, flaky, and flavorful. Its skin can impart a muddy taste, so it's best to remove it before cooking. Smaller pike are somewhat bony but the larger ones can be easily filleted.

NORTHERN PIKE

▶ *It's a Fact:* This hardy fish can withstand long periods of starvation by using its lipid and glycogen reserves instead of body proteins.

Identification: A broad, flat snout; dorsal and anal fins far back on body. Light green to brown on top and sides, underparts whitish or yellowish. Adult has irregular rows of yellow bean-shaped spots on back and side; young has yellow to white wavy bars. State angling record is 38 pounds.

Spawning: Spawn at age 3 to 7. A 25- to 30-pound female may lay up to 500,000 eggs.

Life Span: Older pike are very difficult to age; perhaps up to 25 years.

Food: The very young eat invertebrates; juvenile and mature pike eat mostly fish, including Alaska blackfish, northern pike, whitefishes, sticklebacks, young sockeye salmon, and sheefish.

Habitat and Range: Lakes, rivers, and sloughs. Occur naturally throughout most of Alaska, except lower Alaska Peninsula, Aleutian Islands, parts of Southcentral, and most of Southeast. Illegally introduced into upper Cook Inlet and Kenai Peninsula.

PINK SALMON

The pink salmon—also called humpback and humpy—is the most abundant Pacific salmon in North America and Asia. It has the simplest and shortest life cycle. Upon emerging from the gravel, a young pink migrates quickly to sea, grows rapidly for 18 months, then returns to its river of origin to spawn and die.

Like other salmon, the male pink salmon courts the female while she is digging a nest. He crosses back and forth over her tail area, his body "quivering" the whole time. When the female is ready to deposit her eggs she "crouches" in the nest she has dug, her mouth agape. The male moves alongside and both release their reproductive products while vibrating their tails and anal fins.

The male pink salmon undergoes a remarkable transformation of body shape at maturity. Females and males look alike up to a few weeks before spawning. As the male approaches maturity, however, it develops an enormous hump on its back, a greatly enlarged head, large upper and lower teeth, and a pronounced hook to its snout. Males also become laterally compressed and look very slab-sided. In contrast, the female undergoes only minor changes in body shape.

Biologists believe that the differences that develop between salmon species and sexes allow them to recognize each other and thereby avoid mating with the wrong species. With male pink salmon, however, the changes may help in other ways. The huge hump may prevent the fish from spawning in very shallow water, which may dry up or freeze in winter, killing the eggs. The hump sticking out of the water may also serve as a beacon for predators like bears, distracting them away from the females.

Bears especially like pink salmon. Black bears are known to selectively prey on unspawned female pink salmon to obtain their nutritious eggs. Brown bears often eat only the fat-rich brains of the spawned-out pink salmon, leaving the rest of the carcass for eagles and other creatures. In turn, the pink salmon does not like bears and will show fright responses to bear odor.

Bald eagles also like the pink salmon because it is small enough to be carried to the nest at a time when the eaglets are the largest and hungriest. Also, the pink salmon is usually available when most young eagles leave the nest, about mid-August. Young eagles are inept at obtaining live fish, so a dead or dying pink salmon provides a ready source of nourishment after the parents stop feeding them.

PINK SALMON

▶ *It's a Fact:* Like other salmon, when near its spawning stream, the pink salmon often leaps clear out of the water, sometimes in a rapid series. Reasons for this behavior are unknown.

Identification: Large, black, oval spots on tail. At sea, bright steely blue on top, silvery on sides. At spawning, male is brown to black above with white belly and large hump; female is olive green with dusky patches above, light-colored belly. Juvenile lacks parr marks. Adults average about 4 pounds.

Spawning: Late June to mid-October. Females deposit 1,500 to 2,000 eggs.

Life Span: 2 years.

Food: Young eat zooplankton and larval fishes. Older fish eat zooplankton, squid, and fish.

Habitat and Range: Throughout the North Pacific Ocean and Bering Sea. Spawn in streams along all coastal areas of Alaska, but only occasionally found west of Bering Strait.

RAINBOW TROUT

Alaska is one of the few places left in North America where you can find truly wild stocks of rainbow trout and steelhead. The steelhead is a seagoing rainbow. It migrates hundreds of miles from the streams where it was born, sometimes as far as the coast of Japan. After 1 to 3 years in the ocean, it returns—like salmon—to its home stream to spawn.

The steelhead heads out to sea as a small, 6-inch-long juvenile and returns as a mature adult that may weigh up to 42 pounds. Unlike salmon, many steelhead, especially females, survive to spawn again. After spawning, the ragged, torn, exhausted fish moves slowly downstream and out to sea. Here it begins to heal and restore lost fats. Most will spend at least one winter at sea before returning to spawn again.

Of those that do not go to sea, the Bristol Bay resident rainbow is world famous for its large size. The abundance of sockeye salmon may be the reason. Biologists have found that years when sockeye are abundant, rainbow trout weights are significantly higher than when salmon are less plentiful. Sockeye eggs provide a source of food for young rainbow trout, and decaying carcasses of the spawned-out fish provide nutrients for the insects that the trout feed on.

The Alaska Department of Fish and Game stocks about 100 lakes each year with rainbow trout raised in hatcheries. These lakes are mostly in areas that wild native rainbows do not inhabit, so the hatchery stock doesn't genetically dilute wild stock. One goal of the rainbow stocking program is to ease harvest pressure on wild stocks. The department encourages anglers wishing to eat their catch of rainbow to visit a stocked lake. The state has also passed regulations to close fishing during rainbow spawning times and designated some areas for catch-and-release or trophy fisheries only.

RAINBOW TROUT

▶ *It's a Fact:* This fish is native only to the Pacific slope of North America, but it has been introduced to all continents except Antarctica.

Identification: Difficult to tell from cutthroat trout, but lacks the red to faint yellow slash mark under jaw found on most cutthroat and lacks small teeth on floor of mouth between gill arches. Color variable from blue-green shading to olive on back with black spots on back and most fins. Resident rainbow have pink to red stripe along each side when spawning. Young have 5 to 10 oval parr marks. Distinguished from salmon by 8 to 12 rays in anal fin (salmon have 13 to 19). State angling record for steelhead (and world record) is 42 pounds, 3 ounces. Some stocks of resident rainbow from Bristol Bay average about 23 inches and 5 pounds

at maturity.

Spawning: Late March through early July. Most resident rainbow mature at age 6 or 7; most steelhead mature at age 5 through 7.

Life Span: Up to 11 years.

Food: Insects, fish, and fish eggs in fresh water; a variety of organisms in salt water, especially juvenile greenlings, squids, and amphipods.

Habitat and Range: Resident rainbow trout occur in coastal lakes and streams from Southeast Alaska to Kuskokwim Bay and up Kuskokwim River to Sleetmute. Steelhead occur in coastal streams from Dixon Entrance in Southeast to Cold Bay on Alaska Peninsula.

▲▼▲▼▲▼▲▼▲▼▲▼▲▼▲▼▲▼▲▼▲▼▲▼▲▼▲▼▲▼ ▲▼▲▼

SCULPINS (FRESHWATER)

Slimy sculpin.

There are over 100 species of sculpins in Alaska's waters, but only slimy, prickly, and coastrange sculpins spend most of their time in freshwater. Like sticklebacks, the male sculpin is the more devoted parent. In spring, the male sculpin selects a protected nesting site, such as a cavity under flat-bottomed rocks. The female enters the nest site, deposits her adhesive eggs on the underside of the ceiling rock, and leaves. The male stays on to guard and tend the eggs. He keeps them clean by fanning them with his large pectoral fins, and by removing debris and dead eggs with his mouth. The father is so attentive, he may not even feed until the eggs hatch.

The slimy sculpin is especially territorial and defensive. He will "bark" at intruders by quickly opening and closing his large mouth, and fight to defend his nest. Unlike for most fishes, this behavior is not just a ritual display; the loser of a fight between two male slimy sculpins may be killed.

Sculpins are typically bottom-dwellers, but the very young live near the water's surface. After hatching, the tiny 1/4-inch-long larvae of coastrange and prickly sculpins rise from the bottom and float along with the currents. In lakes, newly hatched sculpins swim up to the surface, remaining there for the next 30 to 35 days. They are especially abundant at the surface during the darkest hours, moving into deeper water during the day. This allows them to feed on tiny plankton, which are most abundant near the lake's surface.

In streams, the sculpin positions itself just downstream from spawning salmon. Here it feeds on aquatic insects and salmon eggs dislodged by spawning activity. It also occasionally feeds on young salmon, but studies have shown its predatory activity is insignificant. Sculpins benefit other fish by providing forage. Sockeye salmon young feed on drifting coastrange sculpin larvae, and the slimy sculpin is major prey for burbot and lake trout.

The slimy sculpin spends all of its time in streams and lakes; prickly and coastrange sculpins occasionally visit estuaries. These fish may be very abundant; a survey of coastrange sculpin estimated 10,000 per $1/2$ mile in one Southeast Alaskan stream.

SLIMY SCULPIN

▶ *It's a Fact:* Like other northern sculpins, this fish is naked—it has no scales. A mucus (slime—hence its name) produced by glands in its skin helps protect it from harmful irritants and lessens drag when it swims.

Identification: Lateral line ends under middle of second dorsal; two pores on tip of chin at midline. Dark brown, green, or dark gray on back and sides with vague mottling or bars below dorsal fin. Breeding males are usually dark, sometimes black with orange edge on front dorsal fin. To 4.7 inches, most not over 3.

Spawning: In spring, shortly after ice breakup.

Females average 150 to over 600 eggs. Several females may lay eggs in one male's nest. Mature at age 2 to 4.

Life Span: Up to 7 years.

Food: Mostly insects; occasionally fish (sometimes their own kind) and fish eggs.

Habitat and Range: Streams and lakes. Most widespread freshwater sculpin in Alaska. Only sculpin in the Interior. Absent from most of Southeast.

▲▼▲▼▲▼▲▼▲▼▲▼▲▼▲▼▲▼▲▼▲▼▲▼▲▼▲▼▲▼▲ ▲▼▲▼

SOCKEYE SALMON

Sockeye is a corruption of the name *sukkai* used by various Indian tribes of southern British Columbia. It is commonly called red salmon by Alaskans because of its deep red flesh and bright red body at spawning time.

Sockeye salmon exhibit more variety in their life history than other Pacific salmon. Most populations are closely tied to lakes. They may spawn along lakeshores or in lake outlets or inlets. The young of some populations may live in streams for a while or migrate to sea soon after emerging from the gravel.

The young sockeye typically spends one or more growing seasons in nursery lakes before migrating to sea. It usually stays near shore during the day and offshore, near the surface, at night. It feeds on insects and zooplankton that migrate from the depths to the surface at night.

Shortly after ice breakup in Alaska in the spring, millions of sockeye smolts head to sea. In Southwestern Alaska, over 60 million leave daily over several days in a mass exodus from Lake Iliamna. They reside in the ocean for 1 to 4 years—usually 2 or 3—before returning to spawn. Sockeye are widely distributed throughout the North Pacific Ocean and Bering Sea, where sockeye from Alaska and Asia feed together.

At sea, the sockeye travels continuously; it may cover over 2,300 miles in one year. As it approaches maturity and its final homeward journey, it speeds up. Biologists have discovered sockeye bound for Bristol Bay average 28 to 35 miles per day during their last 1 to 2 months at sea.

The Bristol Bay watershed in Southwestern Alaska supports the largest number of spawning sockeye in the world. When the sockeye are running, they often form a continuous moving band on both sides of Bristol Bay rivers. On the Kvichak River, biologists often count over 1 million migrating sockeye per day. The total number of sockeye returning to Bristol Bay, before commercial harvests, has exceeded 58 million in recent years.

SOCKEYE SALMON

▶ *It's a Fact:* Sockeye salmon are typically anadromous, but some, over geologic time, have become land-locked and live their entire life cycle in fresh water. These land-locked sockeye salmon are called kokanee.

Identification: No black spots on back or on dorsal and tail fins (unlike pink, coho, and chinook); 28 to 40 long, slender gill rakers and rudiments on first gill arch. At sea, blue-black on top of head and back; silvery sides. At spawning, green heads and bright red bodies. Juveniles have 8 to 14 elliptical to oval parr marks. State angling record is 16 pounds; most range from 4 to 8.

Spawning: Late summer and autumn; some early July and December. Mature at 3 to 5 years. Produce 2,000 to 4,500 eggs (kokanee much less).

Life Span: Up to 5 years. Die after spawning.

Food: Young eat zooplankton and insects. Adults at sea eat zooplankton, larvae, small fish, and occasionally squid.

Habitat and Range: Southeast Alaska north to Kotzebue Sound. Primarily in North Pacific Ocean and Bering Sea; found in limited numbers in Chukchi and Beaufort Seas.

THREESPINE STICKLEBACK

Sticklebacks are tiny fish that have thin bony plates instead of scales on their sides. The threespine stickleback gets its name from the three spines located just in front of its dorsal fin. Two forms of threespine stickleback occur in Alaska—marine and freshwater. The marine form lives in the sea for most of its life, migrating into fresh water or estuaries in spring to breed. In early autumn, the offspring and adults leave the streams and estuaries and move into salt water. Some remain near shore through the winter, while others move to the open sea. Large numbers of threespine sticklebacks have been caught up to 496 miles from shore in the Gulf of Alaska. The freshwater form remains in streams, lakes, and ponds throughout its life.

A male stickleback builds a nest by sucking up sand or mud and depositing it away from the construction site. In the resulting depression, he glues together pieces of vegetation with mucus secreted by his kidneys, until it forms a dome. He then forms a tunnel by wiggling into the structure. He defends the nest by viciously attacking any other breeding male that swims near.

When a female with a belly bulging conspicuously with eggs approaches, the male courts her by zigzagging toward his nest. He repeats this mating dance until the female follows him to the nest, where he points out the entrance with his snout. If the female likes the nest, she will wiggle into the tunnel and deposit between

50 and 100 eggs. The male immediately enters the nest and sheds sperm over them. He may repeat this courtship with several females until his nest is stuffed with eggs.

The male cares for the fertilized eggs and the young. At frequent intervals he fans the nest with his large pectoral fins, creating a flow of water that supplies oxygen to the eggs. The eggs hatch in about 2 weeks. As the young begin emerging from the nest, the male darts about catching them in his mouth and spitting them back into the nest. About 10 days after hatching, the male stops trying to constrain his young, and they begin to disperse.

Sticklebacks are often very abundant and hundreds can be easily scooped up with a small hand seine. Other fish and birds take advantage of this food source. Sticklebacks are an important food of cutthroat trout, Dolly Varden, arctic terns, mergansers, and great blue herons.

THREESPINE STICKLEBACK

▶ *It's a Fact:* When caught by a predator, the stickleback erects and locks its spines in place, which sometimes prevents it from being swallowed.

Identification: Usually 3 spines on back. Marine form has 22 to 37 bony plates along its sides; freshwater form has up to 9. Marine form is bright silver; freshwater form is olive, mottled with distinct bars. At breeding, males turn brilliant colors, including a blue or green eye, bright red or orange underparts, red lining in mouth. To 4 inches.

Spawning: June and July; may breed into August. Female may lay over 1,000 eggs, but deposits only 50 to 200 at one time.

Life Span: Marine form 1 year; freshwater form 2 years.

Food: Zooplankton and insects, sometimes own eggs and young.

Habitat and Range: Mostly lakes, ponds, slow-moving streams, and estuaries containing emergent vegetation. Along the coast of Alaska north to Bristol Bay and Saint Lawrence Island. Found on Arctic coast in one location.

WHITEFISHES

Round whitefish.

Whitefish that live in Alaska's Arctic live and reproduce under especially harsh conditions. Many spawn just about the time when lakes and streams are close to freezing. As is typical of most arctic fish, the whitefish grows slowly, matures late in life, and spawns only every 2 or 3 years.

Eight species of whitefish occur in Alaska: sheefish; broad, humpback, round, and pygmy whitefish; and arctic, Bering, and least ciscos. Sheefish are the largest and, as their name implies, pygmy whitefish are the smallest. Some, such as the humpback whitefish and least cisco, may occur as anadromous, river, or land-locked lake populations. The round and pygmy whitefish are strictly lake- and stream-dwelling fish.

One of the most northerly living whitefish in Alaska—the arctic cisco—has an interesting connection with Canada. The arctic cisco is one of the most abundant and valued subsistence species among anadromous fishes of Alaska's North Slope. Biologists believe that Alaska's cisco spawns in Canada's Mackenzie River and utilizes the river deltas along the North Slope of Alaska (such as the Colville) to feed and overwinter until they reach sexual maturity. Biologists speculate that young ciscos leaving the Mackenzie River get swept into Alaskan waters by the strong westward-flowing ocean currents and cannot return to Canada until they have grown large enough to swim against them.

48

In some lakes of Southwestern Alaska lives the small pygmy whitefish—a glacial relic considered to be the most primitive of the whitefish. This fish seldom grows longer than 10 inches. Two forms of pygmy whitefish have been found in these lakes. One has more gill rakers for straining food from the water, feeds on plankton in mid-water, and often swims with its mouth open, gulping constantly. The other form feeds on bottom organisms and has fewer gill rakers.

Whitefish belong to the same family as salmon, trout, and char, but they have larger scales and small, weak, or absent teeth. The young (except round and pygmy whitefish) do not have the parr marks that distinguish young salmonids. They are especially abundant in the more northerly waters of Alaska and are important as a subsistence food for Alaska's Natives. Whitefish also provide important forage for the predatory fish that live with them.

ROUND WHITEFISH

▶ *It's a Fact:* The whitefish may not feed for 8 to 9 months of the year and must live off stored fat acquired during the short feeding season.

Identification:
Subterminal mouth (opens below front part of head); round in cross section; 74 or more scales along lateral line. Brown to bronze on back; silvery sides, white belly. Juveniles have parr marks (only whitefish in Alaska except pygmy that does). To 20 inches, 3 pounds; most less than 16 inches, 1 pound.

Spawning: Late August in the Arctic, late September to October in Interior, November and December in Southcentral. Female lays 1,000 to 12,000 eggs. Reaches sexual maturity at age 4 or 5 in southern range; age 6, 7, or 8 in northern.

Life Span: 16 years or more.

Food: A bottom feeder on insect larvae and adults, mollusks, fish eggs, and small fish.

Habitat and Range: Lakes, rivers, and streams; throughout Alaska except Yukon–Kuskokwim Delta, Aleutian Islands, Kodiak Island, and most of Southeast except Chilkat, Alsek, and Taku River drainages.

Female kelp greenling, a solitary fish associated with rocks and kelp beds.

CODS

Pacific tomcod.

One way to recognize most codfish is by the little barbel on the end of its chin. It looks a bit like a goatee, but this appendage is not merely decorative; it is a sensory organ that the fish use to explore and taste the bottom for food. A cod, in Alaska's marine waters, is also characterized by a large head, three dorsal fins, and two anal fins.

Most cods are a very important food resource for other fish, birds, marine mammals, and people. One, the Pacific cod, is a major commercial species that is used in fish sticks and fillets. Another, the saffron cod, plays an important role in the subsistence of Alaskan Natives, especially those living along the Bering Sea Coast. Pacific and saffron cods, along with the arctic cod and little Pacific tomcod, are all found in Alaskan waters.

The Pacific cod occurs along the coast of Alaska from Southeast to Norton Sound and throughout the Gulf of Alaska, Aleutian Islands, and eastern Bering Sea. It travels about in schools, usually near the bottom at depths of 150 to 600 feet. This cod grows to over 3 feet long. It spawns in late winter and early spring and a large female produces an incredible number of eggs each year—over 3 million!

The saffron and arctic cods live in our more northerly marine waters. The arctic cod is one of the most abundant species in the Arctic Ocean, where it lives along the edge of the pack ice and hides in cracks in the ice. It is especially cold tolerant and, as it gets older, seems to be most abundant where the water temperature is close to 32°F. This fish is important forage for other fish, seals, beluga whales, narwhals, and seabirds. At one site alone, near Cape Thompson, seabirds consume about 28.6 million pounds of fish—mostly arctic cod—each breeding season.

The saffron cod occurs along the coast north to Kotzebue and in the North Pacific Ocean and Bering and Chukchi Seas. It moves inshore in fall and winter to spawn, at which time coastal Eskimos fish for it by jigging with hand lines strung through holes in the ice. Winter-caught saffron cod is very tasty, but not those caught in the summer.

Pacific tomcod sometimes form huge schools in our marine waters. This fish is a smaller version of the Pacific cod, reaching only about a foot in length. Like the Pacific cod it has three dorsal fins, two anal fins, and a chin barbel. Unlike the Pacific cod, its barbel is shorter, and it does not have spots. Juvenile Pacific tomcod move into shallow waters in summer and fall, whereas the adults usually stay in deeper water at depths of 90 to 720 feet.

PACIFIC TOMCOD

▶ *It's a Fact:* Because of its abundance, wide distribution, and high fecundity, Pacific tomcod (and other cods') eggs, larvae, juveniles, and adult fish are extremely important in the ocean's food web. This species is eaten by lingcod, rockfish, salmon, and marine mammals.

Identification: Very short barbel on chin—its length is about half the diameter of the eye; first anal fin begins below rear of first dorsal fin. Olive green or brownish above, creamy white below. Tips of fins dusky. To 12 inches.

Spawning: Spawns in late winter or spring; some mature by age 2.

Life Span: Unknown.

Food: Shrimp and other invertebrates, small fish.

Habitat and Range: Southeast Alaska to the Bering Sea.

▲▼▲▼▲▼▲▼▲▼▲▼▲▼▲▼▲▼▲▼▲▼▲▼▲▼▲▼▲▼▲ ▲▼▲▼

GREENLINGS

Kelp greenling, male.

Greenlings are a family of fish found only in the North Pacific. These species are rather elongated fish, with only one dorsal fin. Most greenlings have more than one lateral line and a cirrus (fleshy appendage) above each eye. Some species are brightly colored and blend well with the seaweeds and encrusted rocks of their habitat.

The kelp greenling is a striking fish. The female is covered with reddish brown or orange spots, and the male has blue spots ringed with reddish brown. Even its eggs are colorful—a pale blue. The small painted greenling—it grows to 10 inches—is usually whitish with colorful red vertical stripes. This pattern has earned it the nickname "convict fish." Divers say that this fish will follow them around, moving from one rock perch to another like a pet.

Most greenlings are very good eating and are sought by fishermen. The lingcod is one greenling that is especially tasty—meaty and mild. It can be quite a prize for an angler because it can grow up to 5 feet long and 100 pounds. It has an impressively large mouth filled with numerous, sharp canine-like teeth, and comes in a variety of colors—black, brown, blue, and green spotted with orange or yellow. Even its flesh is colored; it is slightly green when raw, but it turns white when cooked.

The lingcod's scientific name, *Ophiodon elongatus,* is quite descriptive of the fish. *Ophiodon*, from the Greek, means "snake tooth," and *elongatus* is Latin for elongated. Its common name, however, makes less sense. The fish is not related to cods, but does somewhat resemble lings (burbot and hakes).

Atka mackerel is a commercial species of greenling that is most abundant around the Aleutian Islands. It grows to 18 inches and about 2 pounds and spawns twice a year, from June through September. You can identify the Atka mackerel by its five lateral lines, forked tail, unnotched dorsal fin, and broad, dark bars on its sides. When mature, the male turns golden yellow or orange with black or brown bars.

All greenlings lay adhesive eggs, usually depositing them in sheltered areas among rocks. The male fiercely guards the eggs and will charge and bite at any intruder including divers. Like other species that lay their eggs in quiet waters, the male greenling must keep water circulating around the eggs in order to maintain a steady supply of oxygen until they hatch. He does this by fanning them with his pectoral fins.

KELP GREENLING

▶ *It's a Fact:* The kelp greenling is a solitary fish; even females tend to live separately from males, except when spawning.

Identification: Five lateral lines, one cirrus above eye, second tiny cirrus midway between eye and dorsal fin. Gray to brownish body, sometimes tinged with copper or blue. Male has blue spots on front of body; yellow inside mouth. Female has small reddish brown or orange spots over entire body. To 21 inches.

Spawning: October to November. Mature at 3 to 5 years.

Life Span: 12 or more years.

Food: Shrimp, crabs, worms, brittle stars, snails, and small fish.

Habitat and Range: Rocky inshore areas, often associated with kelp beds. Southern coastal areas of Alaska to Aleutian Islands.

GUNNELS and PRICKLEBACKS

Crescent gunnel.

There are a lot of gunnel and prickleback species in Alaska's marine waters—32 to be exact. Many of them live in the intertidal zone and you can find them under rocks and seaweed at low tide. As adults they may spend most of their lives in a relatively small area, returning again and again to the same rock. They probably can live for several hours out of water, and you can frequently find them in waterless, moist areas. One, the monkeyface prickleback (not found in Alaska), can survive up to 24 hours out of water.

Gunnels (family Pholididae) and pricklebacks (family Stichaedae) look very much alike but with a few defining differences. All are eel-like fishes with long compressed bodies—most 12 inches or less. Gunnels lack a lateral line, whereas most pricklebacks have at least one. Gunnels usually have a shorter anal fin than pricklebacks. A few species are rather bizarre looking. The decorated warbonnet and mosshead warbonnet—both pricklebacks—have flaps of flesh, called cirri, on the top of their head that resemble a tiny forest of lichens.

These fish are often very colorful, and individuals of the same species may vary in color. The penpoint gunnel—noted for its large, pen-shaped anal spine—varies its color depending on its diet and environment. It may be camouflaged green through brown to red, blending in with the surrounding algae or eelgrass.

Gunnels and pricklebacks lay their eggs under or among rocks or shells. The female high cockscomb—noted for a fleshy crest on its head—guards her eggs by bending her body around the egg mass. She fans them continuously by undulating the posterior part of her body. The eggs hatch in about 3 weeks into tiny larvae less than 1/3 inch long.

The shallow-water habitat frequented by these fish makes them easy prey for fish-eating birds and mammals. I have watched great blue herons catch one after another, especially at twilight when the fish venture out to feed. When photographing belted kingfishers bringing food to their nest, I noted that gunnels and pricklebacks were frequent fare. Because they are easy to find and capture, they could also be important survival food for humans stranded or lost along Alaska's rocky coastline. They are reported to be good eating.

CRESCENT GUNNEL

▶ *It's a Fact:* This gunnel's scientific name, *Pholis laeta,* comes from the Greek *pholas* which means "one who lies in wait," and the Latin *laeta,* which means "joyful."

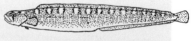

Identification: Black, crescent-shaped marks at base of dorsal fin. Yellowish green with slight mottling on its side. In winter, mature male is orange or reddish on cheeks, throat, pectoral fins, and ventral region. To 10 inches.

Spawning: January and February. Eggs white to creamy. Deposits 600 to 1,600 eggs in an adhesive rounded mass.

Life Span: Unknown.

Food: Unknown, but probably includes small crustaceans, such as amphipods, and marine worms.

Habitat and Range: At low tide, look in tide pools filled with seaweed and under the larger encrusted rocks. Found along the coast from Southeast to Aleutians and Bering Sea.

PACIFIC HALIBUT

The halibut undergoes one of nature's most extraordinary transformations early in life. When newly hatched, the $^1/_3$-inch-long larval halibut has a huge yolk sac attached to an ordinary upright little body. Within days, at about 1 inch long, one eye starts to migrate across the snout to the other side of the head until it lies next to the other one, and the mouth twists around at an angle. At the same time, the fish's body flattens out from an upright, rounded shape and pigmentation on the underside fades to white. Eventually, it is lying and swimming with one side up and one side down.

Pacific halibut spawn in deep water from 600 to 1,500 feet. The fertilized eggs drift with the ocean currents and hatch in about 15 days. The young halibut is heavier than the surface seawater and drifts about with the ocean currents. As it grows, its specific gravity decreases and it gradually rises toward the surface. In 6 to 7 months it is carried inshore by surface currents and settles on the ocean floor.

For about three years, the young halibut remain in shallow inshore waters. As they grow older, they move into deeper waters and migrate east and south. Young halibut tagged in the Bering Sea and the western Gulf of Alaska have migrated as far south as British Columbia, Washington, and Oregon. Biologists suspect these fish were spawned in these areas. Older halibut typically move from deep water along the edge of the continental shelf, where they spend the winter, to shallow coastal waters with depths of 90 to 900 feet for the summer.

Fishermen still catch halibut the way they did 100 years ago. They use longline gear, developed in the late 1800s, which consists of 1,800-foot lengths of leaded groundline called skates. Hooks on lines called gangions are attached to the skates about 18 feet apart. The skates are strung together in a set, which is anchored at the bottom and tied to a buoy at the surface. The hooks are baited with herring or other fish and octopus. The joint Canadian-U.S. International Pacific Halibut Commission, established in 1923 to manage and direct research on this fish, determines annual commercial fishing seasons, area closures, and quotas.

PACIFIC HALIBUT

▶ *It's a Fact:* This bottom-dwelling fish is a strong swimmer. Unlike other, more sedentary flatfish, it often leaves the seafloor to feed on pelagic fish, such as sand lance and herring, which swim closer to the surface.

Identification: Eyes usually on right side; tail slightly indented; lateral line arched over pectoral fin; jaw extends only to middle of eye. Dark brown or gray with pale marbling on eyed side; white on blind underside. State angling record is 440 pounds. Females to 8 feet, 500 pounds; males to 4 feet, 120 pounds.

Spawning: November to January. The male matures at about age 8; the female at age 12. A 250-pound female may produce 4 million eggs yearly.

Life Span: Up to 42 years. Most commercially caught halibut range from 8 to 15 years old.

Food: Fish, such as cod, Pacific sand lance, and Pacific herring, and crabs, clams, squids, and other invertebrates.

Habitat and Range: Found over a variety of bottom types along the Pacific Coast to the Bering Sea as far as Norton Sound. Young usually near shore, adults in deeper water, to about 3,600 feet.

PACIFIC HERRING

When Pacific herring spawn you usually know it. Occurring in schools of sometimes up to 1 million or more fish in nearshore areas, the spawning males turn the water white with milt. From an airplane this milky water can be seen from miles away. Their presence is also signalled by hundreds of bald eagles, Steller sea lions, harbor seals, and an occasional humpback whale that comes to feast on the fish.

Millions of herring eggs never hatch. Those laid within the intertidal area are exposed at low tide, and if the weather is warm and sunny they may dehydrate and die. During storms, the seaweeds covered with eggs may be torn from the bottom and cast high upon the beach, causing further mortality.

Biologists estimate 50 to 99 percent of all herring eggs die from natural causes or are eaten before they hatch. Snails, crabs, fish, ravens, ducks, and other birds eat the eggs. Jellyfish, young salmon, and other animals eat those that do hatch while they are still larvae or juveniles. Adult herring are eaten by just about every fish and sea mammal large enough to eat them. In fact, so many are eaten that only about 1 adult per 10,000 eggs returns to spawn.

When spawning, the female turns on her side and, with fins extended, body rigid, and tail vibrating, she moves slowly forward, brushing the substrate with her vent. She lays her adhesive eggs in large masses on seaweed fronds, rocks, and pilings. She may take several days to release all her eggs. During this time, the males swim at random among the spawning females and release their milt.

The egg hatches in about 10 to 21 days (depending on water temperature) into a 1/4-inch-long transparent larva that drifts and swims with the ocean currents for about 6 to 8 weeks. At a length of about 2½ inches the larva changes to a juvenile herring that resembles a miniature adult, complete with scales. The juvenile resides and feeds in sheltered bays and inlets for 3 or 4 years, where it appears to be segregated from adult populations until it reaches maturity.

After spawning, adult herring often move in schools offshore to feed on zooplankton and small fish. The herring schools may spend the daylight hours near the bottom and move toward the surface in the evening to feed. Throughout the summer and fall, a herring feeds voraciously to accumulate enough fat reserves to tide it over the winter. Apparently it feeds little in winter, because most herring examined at this time have empty stomachs.

PACIFIC HERRING

▶ *It's a Fact:* This species is harvested commercially for roe, fillets, and bait. Herring sac roe, especially eggs laid on kelp, is a great delicacy in Japan and commands a high price.

Identification: Pelvic fin under dorsal fin. No spines, adipose fin, or spots. Large scales, easily removed. Silver sides and belly; bluish green to olive on top. Maximum length 9 to 18 inches.

Spawning: Late March to late June. Mature at age 3 or 4, spawn every year thereafter. Females lay about 10,000 eggs at age 3 and nearly 60,000 by age 8.

Life Span: About 10 years in Southeast, up to 18 years in Bering Sea.

Food: Zooplankton, such as copepods and euphausiids, and small fish.

Habitat and Range: Shallow vegetated areas in bays and estuaries when spawning in spring, deeper water in fall and winter. Occurs throughout the Gulf of Alaska and the Bering and Chukchi Seas.

PACIFIC SAND LANCE

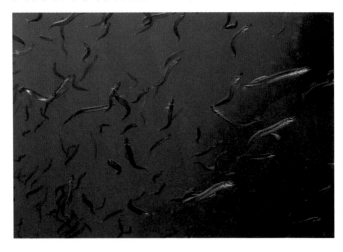

Watching a sand lance is fun. When startled, it dives head-first into the sand. Then, wiggling upward in an arc, it pokes its head out to look around. If you move suddenly, it wiggles tailfirst back into the substrate until it is completely covered. Sometimes, as you walk about in the shallows, the sand lance panics, squirts out of the sand, rushes madly about, then dives back in. If you grab one, hang on or it will disappear in a flash.

Burying itself in sand is not just a trick, it is an important survival technique. Like many other species, the sand lance does not have a swim bladder, an organ that gives fish natural buoyancy. Unless it moves constantly, it sinks to the bottom. To conserve energy and escape from predators, the sand lance buries itself completely at night. During the winter, when food supplies such as zooplankton are low, it spends most of the time resting in the substrate. This enables it to efficiently metabolize fat reserves stored up during the summer and allows its gonads to mature in preparation for spawning.

The Pacific sand lance is one of the most important fish in our marine waters. When the food habits of fish-eating birds, mammals, and other fish are studied, the sand lance usually shows up as the major item on the menu. Pink, coho, chinook, and sockeye salmon all eat sand lance, as do halibut, cod, Dolly Varden, and even herring, which feed on their larvae. The sand lance is also the most important fish in the diet of nesting marbled murrelets and a major food of kittiwakes, murres, puffins, and seals.

Look for sand lance along sandy beaches and sandy intertidal sloughs at or near low tide, especially where there is a feeding frenzy of gulls, terns, and bald eagles. The larger gulls usually alight on the water and jab for the sand lances, while arctic terns and smaller Bonaparte's gulls hover and plunge after their prey. Eagles may swoop and snatch them from the water in their talons or stand alongside a water-filled pocket in the sand, waiting patiently for one to emerge. Crows and ravens dig for them in the sand with a sideways motion of their bills. They seem very successful at digging them out, perhaps to the amazement of nearby gulls.

PACIFIC SAND LANCE

▶ *It's a Fact:* The mechanism that causes sand lance to enter sand for the winter may be related to fat content and environmental factors, such as decreasing food, water temperature, and day length.

Identification: Lower jaw longer than upper jaw; pointed snout; long dorsal fin with no spines; no pelvic fins; forked tail fin; lateral line high on back. Iridescent or metallic blue or green above, silvery below. To 10 1/2 inches.

Spawning: October (at Kodiak), and perhaps other times, on the surface of sand. Mature at age 2 or 3.

Life Span: Probably up to age 5, but not well known.

Food: Larvae feed on phytoplankton, invertebrate eggs, and larvae; juveniles and adults feed on zooplankton.

Habitat and Range: Occurs in large schools in a variety of habitats—nearshore areas, channels, within beach sand, and offshore areas. Stays near surface when over deep water. Pacific Ocean, Bering Sea, Chukchi Sea.

PACIFIC VIPERFISH

Viperfish, Chauliodus sp.

The Pacific viperfish is one of the many bizarre creatures that frequent the great depths of Alaska's marine waters. It possesses qualities that distinguish deep-sea fish from the more familiar shallow-water inhabitants, including luminous organs called photophores. A single fish may have hundreds or even thousands of these brightly colored light organs. Their purpose is not well known, but they may be a way for species to recognize their own kind and for males and females to tell each other apart, especially at night or in the dark depths of the sea. Photophores also help camouflage the fish. From its ventral photophores the viperfish can match the light coming from above, making it less visible to predators from below. They may also be used to attract food.

The Pacific viperfish has huge fang-like teeth that are unequal in length. Some teeth have tiny barbs at their end, which help the fish hold onto prey. To accommodate its huge teeth, the viperfish has a wide mouth with strong jaws that can deliver a vicious snap and bite.

The viperfish has another odd feature, a long, string-like structure that dangles in front of its mouth and has a luminescent organ at its tip. This appendage is actually the first ray of its dorsal fin. Some scientists believe it acts like a phony fish lure, attracting prey within snatching range.

Like some other deep-sea fish, the viperfish often migrates

vertically at night, swimming upward from the depths toward the surface. This movement is probably a way to partake of the more abundant food in surface waters.

Another deep-sea fish that has photophores along its body is the northern lampfish. It is one of the most abundant deep-sea fish in our waters, and like the viperfish moves up and down in the water column to feed. At night, lampfish ascend in such large numbers that other creatures take advantage of their presence and feed on them. The lampfish is extremely high in lipids and provides its predators with over twice the food energy of most other forage fishes. In the Pribilof Islands, where over 90 percent of the world's population of red-legged kittiwakes nest, biologists found the northern lampfish to be critical to the nesting success of these birds. Lampfish are also a main item in the diet of Steller sea lions around these islands.

Most deep-sea fish breed at great depths, but their eggs are buoyant and float at the surface, where they and the recently hatched young become part of the plankton. Only later, after the larvae have transformed into juveniles, do they move into the depths of the ocean.

PACIFIC VIPERFISH

▶ *It's a Fact:* The light produced by the luminescent photophores in Pacific viperfish comes from gland cells. In some other deep-sea fish, light comes from bioluminescent bacteria that live on the fish, rather than the fish itself.

Identification: Long, fang-like teeth; two rows of photophores along posterior part of body; dorsal and ventral adipose fins. Dark brown to black. To 10 inches.
Spawning: Unknown.
Life Span: To 8 years.

Food: Small planktonic crustaceans, arrow worms, and fish—sometimes as big as or bigger than themselves.
Habitat and Range: At depths of 500 to 2,000 feet. Found throughout the Pacific Ocean and Bering Sea.

ROCKFISHES

Yelloweye rockfish, adult.

Rockfishes come in a variety of colors—from drab to brilliant. Those living near the surface are mostly brownish hues, while those living in deep water are predominantly red or orange. The deep dwellers can wear brighter colors because the characteristics of light in water allow them to remain inconspicuous. Because red and orange are long waves located at the end of the light spectrum, they are the first colors to be absorbed by the water so they don't penetrate very deep. Thus a red or orange rockfish residing below this range of wavelength penetration cannot reflect light and appears black to its potential enemies.

There are 35 species of rockfishes (genus *Sebastes*) found in Alaska's marine waters. These fish are known for their tasty flesh; in markets, you may find rockfish—especially yelloweye—labeled as red snapper. The most commonly caught species in Alaska are the Pacific ocean perch and the northern, rougheye, shortraker, dusky, yelloweye, and quillback rockfish.

We do not know exactly how rockfishes mate. However, we do know that the female rockfish is ovoviviparous—that is, the eggs are fertilized internally, develop and hatch inside the mother's body, and remain there until the yolk sac is absorbed. Most rockfish young are less than 1/2 inch long when they are born.

Like most fish, the rockfish has an air bladder, a hollow organ near the top of the body cavity that keeps it weightless so it can swim easily. In rockfish, the air bladder obtains its gases from the blood rather than through a tube connected to the esophagus as in most other fish. When swimming upward at a normal speed, air in the bladder is gradually drawn out by the blood to compensate for changes in pressure, which decreases closer to the surface. If a rockfish surfaces too quickly—for example, when hooked by a fisherman and dragged up fast—it cannot change its pressure quickly enough so its bladder expands and forces the stomach out its mouth. Fishermen waste a lot of rockfish this way. When seeking other fish, they throw unwanted rockfish back in the water. Unable to recover from the sudden pressure change, it dies.

Rockfish populations can be easily overharvested and even wiped out by fishing. Many populations live their entire lives in one area. Hence, when overexploited, the population is not easily replenished by stocks from other areas. One study in Southeast Alaska showed some populations spent their entire lives near an underwater shipwreck. When biologists caught the fish and moved them to another site, like homing pigeons they came back.

YELLOWEYE ROCKFISH

▶ *It's a Fact:* This fish is among the longest lived of all fishes.

Identification: Rasp-like ridge of spines above each eye. Adult has bright yellow eyes and is golden yellow or orange, usually with 1 light stripe along lateral line. Juvenile is red with 2 white stripes on side. To 3 feet; juveniles to 1 foot. State angling record is 26 pounds.

Spawning: First reproduce at age 12 to 15. The female releases up to 2 million tiny fish between January and May.

Life Span: To 114 years.

Rockfish about 2 feet long may be 40 to 80 years old.

Food: Juveniles eat primarily plankton, such as copepods and fish eggs. Adults eat smaller rockfish, Pacific sand lance, Pacific herring, cod, and crustaceans.

Habitat and Range: Around reefs and boulder piles at depths of 450 to 600 feet. Occur in the Gulf of Alaska and throughout Southeast.

SABLEFISH

The Gustavus Inn at Glacier Bay in Southeast Alaska serves a delicious ginger-steamed sablefish. The inn's owners, David and Jo Ann Lesh, have graciously given me permission to reprint their recipe, so here it is:

Place sablefish fillet skin-side down in a shallow baking pan. Sprinkle each fillet with 1 tablespoon Japanese soy sauce, 1 tablespoon dry white wine, and 1 teaspoon sugar. Spread with julienned fresh ginger and thinly sliced green onions. Cover tightly with foil and bake at 400°F until the thickest part of the fillet reaches 130°F on an instant-reading thermometer. To prepare a sauce to serve on the side, drain the liquid from the fish into a sauté pan and add a small amount of cornstarch to thicken.

Once you taste this fish, you'll know why it is an important commercial species. Fishermen catch it in trawls, traps, and on longlines. Much of the catch is marketed in Japan, where it is popular as sashimi because of its high oil content. It is also sold fresh and frozen and is excellent smoked.

The sablefish travels about in schools. The adults and older juveniles reside on or near the bottom over sand or mud (most adults at depths between 1,300 and 3,300 feet). The young-of-the-year juvenile is pelagic and occurs in surface and nearshore waters to depths of 500 feet. Most adult sablefish do not migrate great distances, although some tagged as juveniles have migrated over 2,000 miles in 6 or 7 years. One tagged off Washington State was recovered at the tip of the Aleutian Islands.

The sablefish spawns near the edge of the continental shelf. The eggs float about at depths below 650 feet. When they hatch, in about 2 to 3 weeks, the tiny larvae swim immediately to the water surface. The larvae begin feeding on zooplankton, such as copepods, and grow rapidly—about $1/8$ inch per day. Sablefish are important forage for other marine fish, such as Pacific cod, Pacific halibut, and lingcod; seabirds, which are attracted to abundant young sablefish in nearshore surface waters; and marine mammals. Killer whales have been reported to selectively feed on sablefish caught on longlines, ignoring other species.

SABLEFISH

▶ *It's a Fact:* Sablefish is often marketed under the name blackcod. However, it is not a cod, nor is it closely related.

Identification: A streamlined fish with 2 dorsal fins, 1 anal fin directly below second dorsal. Adult is dark gray, greenish gray, or black, usually with paler blotches or chainlike pattern on back. Young is blue-black above and white below, occasionally all yellow, white, or other color. To 44 inches and over 126 pounds; most less than 30 inches and 25 pounds.

Spawning: At depths of 900 to 2,500 feet from January through March. Mature at age 4 to 6 (20 to 24 inches). A 20-inch female produces about 100,000 eggs per season; a 40-inch female may produce 1 million eggs.

Life Span: Up to 55 years.

Food: Invertebrates, squid, and small fish, such as Pacific herring and rockfish. Larger ones eat mostly fish.

Habitat and Range: Young near surface and inshore waters; adults near bottom. Throughout Gulf of Alaska, along Aleutian Islands, and at edge of continental slope in eastern Bering Sea.

SCULPINS (SALTWATER)

Grunt sculpin.

Sculpins have some of the most unusual habits of any Alaskan fish. For example, the Pacific staghorn sculpin hums when under stress. Attempt to take one from your hook and you may feel the vibration from its humming. The male fourhorn sculpin, when defending its territory, also produces a low-pitched humming sound with a frequency of about 125 cycles per second. Another species, the tiny grunt sculpin, gets its name from the grunting and hissing sounds it makes when removed from the water.

The grunt sculpin is an active little fish that appears to jump and crawl on the bottom. The female chases males until she traps one in a rock crevice. She keeps him there until she lays her eggs.

A mature male scalyhead sculpin has a well-developed, penis-like appendage that it uses to fertilize the female internally. Sculpin eggs are often brightly colored—green, blue, yellow, orange, pink, red—perhaps to warn off predators as at least some eggs are known to be poisonous. This is a form of protective coloration among many species, which use bright colors like an alarm that says "don't touch."

Several species of sculpins scoot about on the rocks and sit propped up on their large pectoral fins. Marine species live in tide pools or in shallow or deep marine waters. Most species range in length from 2 to 10 inches, but a few, such as the great sculpin, may reach a length of 2$^{1}/_{2}$ feet.

Sculpins are among the most abundant fishes in Alaska; over 100 sculpin species occur in our marine waters. Along the Beaufort Sea coast in Northern Alaska, biologists estimate that fourhorn sculpins account for more than 69 percent of all fish found. Pacific staghorn sculpins are also abundant. Fishermen seem to catch them more frequently than any other species of fish, especially if their bait nears the bottom.

Sculpins benefit other fish, birds, and mammals by providing food for them. The abundance of young Pacific staghorn sculpins in shallow intertidal areas makes them easy prey for birds, including greater yellowlegs, great blue herons, arctic terns, and common mergansers. In deeper water, cormorants, seals, sea lions, and river otters also feed on these sculpins.

Sculpins are also a potentially good source of food for humans. The staghorn sculpin's abundance, ease of capture in shallow waters, relatively large size (up to 18 inches) and edibility make it an excellent source of food for survival for anyone stranded along Alaska's coast. Foragers should be aware, however, that this fish's eggs are poisonous.

GRUNT SCULPIN

▶ *It's a Fact:* The grunt sculpin's eyes each operate independently, so it can watch for danger or prey in two directions at once.

Identification: Short snout; large head; long, individually separated rays in pectoral fin. Yellowish to tan body streaked with brown, red at base of tail, reddish fin rays. To 3 inches.

Spawning: In winter. Female lays yellow to orange eggs.

Life Span: Unknown.

Food: Young eat zooplankton and invertebrate and fish larvae. Older fish also eat crustaceans.

Habitat and Range: Tide pools and shallow rocky coasts from Southeast to the Bering Sea. Also has been found over sand and to depths of 500 feet.

SKATES

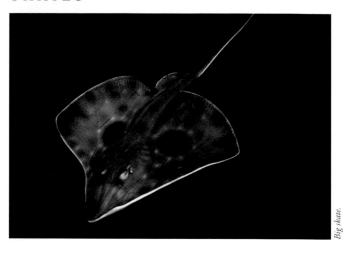

Big skate.

The skate is a bizarre creature that looks like a space ship or a stealth bomber. Its pectoral fins form the shape of a disk, which radiates outward from the body. To swim, the skate undulates the edges of these disk-like wings, moving slowly along just above the muddy bottom where it lives. It can travel very fast, but most of the time it lies motionless on the bottom.

The skate belongs to a class of fishes that are the oldest surviving group of jawed vertebrates, the cartilaginous fish. Its skeleton is made of cartilage—a translucent material-—rather than the calcified bones of most other fishes. For at least 400 million years, these fishes have been a successful part of the marine ecosystem. Skates diverged from the sharks, another cartilaginous fish, in the early Jurassic period, about 180 million years ago.

The skate has gills, like most other fish, with openings on the ventral side of its body. But a skate also has two fairly large openings on its head, called spiracles, just behind its eyes. Most of the water that eventually flows over its gills enters through the spiracles instead of through its mouth as in most other fish. This allows the skate to breathe while partially buried in mud or just resting on the bottom.

The skate has unique breeding behavior. Prior to mating, a female skate continuously rubs the anal region of the male with her tail and body. This causes a reflex erection of the male's claspers, modified pelvic fins that he uses to grasp and fertilize her. The male inserts his claspers into the female's body cavity and ejects his sperm internally.

Special glands within the female secrete a tough, horny envelope around the fertilized eggs. After several months the female deposits the egg cases onto the ocean floor. They are quite distinctive, and we sometimes see them on beaches or brought up in bottom trawlnets. Typically rectangular in shape, they usually have prominent horns at the corners. Some species' egg cases have long curly tendrils that wrap around seaweed and anchor them to the substrate. After several months, a baby skate emerges that looks just like a miniature adult.

About 22 species of skate have been found in Alaska's marine waters. One, the Alaska skate, is only found here. Another common species is the big skate—a huge fish up to 8 feet long. The sides of this fish's disk are edible; they taste amazingly similar to scallops. At least 5 species of skates are caught in commercial bottom trawls.

BIG SKATE

▶ *It's a Fact:* This skate deposits a large, foot-long egg case. It is the only skate that produces multiple embryos per case—from 2 to 7 each.

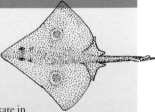

Identification: Shallow notch in rear edge of each pelvic fin (other species have deep notches). Long snout. On top, gray, brown, reddish brown, olive brown, black, often with white spotting and darker mottling. Has two prominent eyespots on top that look like the large end of binoculars (hence species name *binoculata*). Largest skate in Alaska—to 8 feet; most under 6 feet, 200 pounds.

Spawning: Not well known; perhaps any month of the year.

Life Span: Unknown.

Food: Crustaceans and fish.

Habitat and Range: Most common at depths of 10 to 360 feet. Southeast Alaska, Gulf of Alaska, Bering Sea.

SOLES and FLOUNDERS

Starry flounder.

Soles and flounders undergo the unusual metamorphosis of all flatfish. After hatching they swim upright for a while, then one eye, usually the left, moves across the head next to the other eye. Although most flatfish eyes end up on the right side, the eyes of the petrale sole are on its left side. Starry flounders can't seem to make up their minds—both right- and left-sided fish are common. Eventually, the underside of the fish turns white, and the top side turns shades of gray and brown. These fish are so good at camouflage, they can change color to match the pattern of sand or gravel they rest on.

Flatfish are rather unexciting fish. Many spend most of their lives just lying around on the bottom waiting for a meal to wander within range. But they do have some interesting quirks. The starry flounder can curl its long dorsal and anal fins toward the bottom and crawl about on its fin rays like a multilegged caterpillar. Dover sole observed in an aquarium would swim over to the side, stand up on their tails, and stick their faces against the glass, looking for "all the world like pop-eyed flying squirrels."(Love, 1991)

Most flatfish hunt for their food along the bottom. Some surprise unsuspecting clams and bite off their siphons while they are extended above the substrate to feed. Some species, such as the Pacific sanddab, may hunt for food well above the bottom, especially at night.

Female flatfish produce a huge number of eggs—sometimes millions. Most flatfish eggs are lighter than seawater, so they tend to rise and float near the surface. Rock sole eggs are an exception—they sink and stick to the bottom until hatching. In Alaska, rock sole are fished commercially for the roe, which is worth over $25 million in some years.

Flatfish are fished commercially in the Gulf of Alaska and eastern Bering Sea. In the Bering Sea the most important species are yellowfin sole, Greenland turbot, arrowtooth flounder, and rock sole. In the Gulf of Alaska, arrowtooth flounder, flathead sole, rock sole, rex sole, Dover sole, yellowfin sole, and starry flounder are taken commercially. Native peoples living in coastal communities catch flatfish as a subsistence food.

STARRY FLOUNDER

▶ *It's a Fact:* Flounder eggs are tiny—less than 1 millimeter in diameter. At hatching the larvae are only $1/8$ inch long and float upside down because of their relatively large, buoyant yolk sac.

Identification: Dorsal and anal fins marked with dark and white to orange bars. Very rough surface caused by modified scales (called stellate tubercles) with well-developed spines. Eyed side is dark brown to nearly black with occasional greenish tinge. To 3 feet and 20 pounds.

Spawning: Late winter and spring. Most males mature at age 2, females at 3. An average-sized female may contain 11 million eggs.

Life Span: Up to 24 years. Females live longer than males.

Food: Young feed on plankton. Larger fish eat clams, snails, starfish, polychaete worms, crabs, mysids, and nemerteans. The very large flounders will eat fish.

Habitat and Range: Inshore waters, estuaries, sometimes up rivers in summer; deeper water in winter. Some found in deeper water all year. Coastal areas of Alaska except Arctic Ocean.

SPOTTED RATFISH

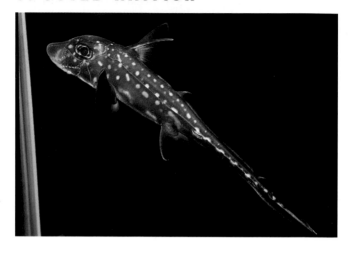

The spotted ratfish belongs to a group of living fossils called chimaeras, which have changed little from ancient times. Chimaeras are described in Homer's *Iliad* as female monsters with a lion's forepart, a goat's middle, and a dragon's hind end. The spotted ratfish does appear to be made up of several different creatures—it has a large rabbit-like head, huge green eyes, forward-facing chisel-like teeth, and a body that tapers back to a remarkably long, rat-like tail, which accounts for its common name. Its scientific name, *Hydrolagus colliei*, means "water rabbit."

And that is only the beginning! Its head is covered with prominent, highly sensitive lateral line canals, and it has a venomous spine in front of its dorsal fin. A male ratfish has an unusual device called a tenaculum attached to its head. It is a cartilaginous, club-like appendage armed with prickles and can be folded into a pit on its head. The male uses the tenaculum to grasp or stimulate the female during mating. A male also has sharp clasping organs on either side of his vent, which can give you a nasty cut.

A graceful swimmer, the ratfish moves like a slow-flying bird, flapping its huge pectoral fins. Its tail, which is almost finless, is of little value for locomotion. Its skin is smooth and scaleless, but when pulled out of the water its soft body sags and it loses its sleek appearance. Ratfish are attracted to lights at night and occasionally become trapped in tide pools. But mostly, they are only seen by commercial fishermen, especially trawlers, and the occasional sport angler who accidentally snags one by its large pectoral fins.

The spotted ratfish conducts elaborate courtship maneuvers, during which the male undergoes a striking change in color. The female extrudes two eggs at a time, each contained in a 5-inch-long, ridged brown capsule that has stiff hairlike bristles along the edge. She may take up to 30 hours to finally extrude her egg cases, which then hang from her body on a long filament for another 4 to 6 days. The egg cases end up planted vertically in the mud or just lying with filaments entangled in the bottom.

The ratfish is edible, although it is rather bland and leaves an unpleasant aftertaste. This fish is eaten by sharks, Pacific halibut, and pigeon guillemots, but its eggs are toxic. Historically, before the use of synthetics, ratfish livers were processed into fine oils for lubricating machinery.

SPOTTED RATFISH

▶ *It's a Fact:* This fish seeks its food by smell and by sensing the vibration of prey through its elaborate lateral line canals—a system capable of "distant touch."

Identification: Easy—with its large rabbit-like head and long tapering body, no other fish in Alaska looks like it! Body usually brown; sometimes silvery with iridescent shades of gold, green, and blue; always with white spots. To 38 inches.

Spawning: Females may extrude eggs year-round. Age at maturity unknown (no one knows how to age them).

Life Span: Unknown.

Food: Fish, clams, mussels, shrimp, worms, and starfish.

Habitat and Range: Usually near bottom at depths below 240 feet; occasionally along shore in shallow waters. Found in Southeast Alaska.

WALLEYE POLLOCK

Walleye pollock comprise the largest single-species commercial fishery in the world. The reasons are threefold: pollock roe has become very popular in Japan; the fish is now used as a substitute for the depleted stocks of cod and haddock in the Atlantic and made into frozen fillets or fish sticks; and, perhaps most important, it is used to make surimi (imitation shellfish).

To make surimi the walleye pollock is filleted, minced, and thoroughly washed in chilled water to remove blood, fat, and enzymes and increase certain elastic proteins. The water is then pressed out, leaving an odorless, white substance that has a texture similar to crab meat. To make the final product—simulated shellfish—color and flavors are added.

Robin Love, in his delightful book *Probably More Than You Want to Know About the Fishes of the Pacific Coast,* calls surimi "pretend seafood." It is a pretty good facsimile of the real thing—and much more affordable.

Human demand for the exotic roe, fish sticks, and surimi competes directly with some other creatures. For example, walleye pollock comprise over half the diet of the Steller sea lions in the Gulf of Alaska. The pollock are smaller now, and biologists believe the sea lions are suffering nutritional stress as a result. Also, common murres on the Seward Peninsula have decreased in proportion to the increased harvests of walleye pollock in the south-eastern Bering Sea. While these cause-and-effect relationships have not been proven, the evidence seems more than circumstantial.

Many other fish species also like to eat pollock, especially young pollock. Some even anticipate the annual arrival of each new crop of pollock and lie in wait for them. In Southeast Alaska, biologists using scuba gear would observe great sculpins lining up in rows just before the small pollock arrived. The sculpin would gorge themselves on pollock until their bellies bulged. For 22 consecutive years the biologists observed a consistent pattern of timing, location, and depth by the young-of-the-year walleye pollock—a consistency that sculpins apparently learned, too. The same pattern appears to occur in the Bering Sea.

WALLEYE POLLOCK

▶ *It's a Fact:* Its scientific name, *Theragra*, comes from two Greek words—*ther*, meaning "beast," and *agra*, which means "food"—and refers to its importance as food for sea mammals, such as fur seals.

Identification:
3 well-separated dorsal fins, anus below space between first and second dorsal fins, slightly projecting lower jaw. Some have a tiny chin whisker. Silvery sides, olive green to brown above, often with faint blotches or mottling. Young has 2 or 3 narrow yellow bands on sides. To 3 feet, 11 pounds.

Spawning: February to early May in Bering Sea; late March and April in Gulf of Alaska. Mature at age 3 to 6. Eggs and sperm broadcast in mid-water at depths of 300 to 750 feet. Females produce from 20,000 to 1.7 million eggs each year.

Life Span: Up to 31 years, most less than 18 in Bering Sea and 11 in Gulf of Alaska.

Food: Very young eat copepods; euphausiids, small shrimp, capelin, Pacific sand lance, Pacific herring, and young salmon. Highly cannibalistic on its own young.

Habitat and Range: Over the continental shelf, mostly at depths between 300 and 1,000 feet. Center of abundance is Bering Sea and Gulf of Alaska.

WOLFFISHES

Wolf-eel, male.

Wolffishes are fearsome-looking creatures. Two species live in Alaska, the Bering wolffish and the wolf-eel. Both species have long, tapering, eel-like bodies and ferocious-looking teeth: sharp conical canines for tearing and flat heavy molars for crunching. And crunch they do. These fish can easily chomp through the hard shells of crabs, clams, and snails. After eating, the wolf-eel rubs itself against the bottom, perhaps to scatter the broken shells of its prey.

A large wolf-eel can inflict painful bites on humans, too. When it is under stress, such as when it is hooked at the end of a line or caught in a net or trap, you should be wary of its powerful mouth. However, if you are fortunate enough to encounter one in its natural habitat, you can tame and even hand-feed it. Sometimes, wolf-eels tamed by divers will swim out of their cave to greet anyone who approaches.

An old wolf-eel is really weird looking. I think its head resembles some of the characters I used to make out of shrunken potatoes when I was a kid. Especially a mature male—it has a whitish, lumpy head with large pouched cheeks. A mature female is darker and not so puffy looking about the head. The juvenile, however, is a sleek and beautiful fish, sometimes colored orange.

Despite its looks, the wolf-eel has a tasty, white, flaky flesh. Its tough skin can be tanned and made into leather. Some coastal

Indians once valued the wolf-eel, believing that it had curative attributes. They called it the "doctor fish," but only medicine men were allowed to eat it. They believed it enhanced their healing powers.

When courting, the male wolf-eel butts his head against the female's abdomen, wraps around her, and fertilizes her eggs as she extrudes them. She lays 10,000 or more eggs in a single mass, then they both wrap themselves around the egg mass to protect it. Only one of them at a time leaves the eggs to feed. The female periodically rotates the eggs until they hatch 13 to 16 weeks later.

The juvenile wolf-eel swims about in the upper part of the ocean for up to 2 years. It then settles to the bottom and actively swims about for a while. Eventually it finds a shelter among the rocks and becomes sedentary.

WOLF-EEL

▶ *It's a Fact:* A male and female may pair for life. They will occupy the same cave until driven out by other wolf-eels or a large octopus.

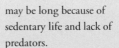

Identification: Eel-like body, stout teeth, no pelvic fins or lateral line. Most are gray to brown, some greenish. Round dark spots over body surrounded by pale rings. Older fish may be more mottled. Young often orangish with stripes toward tail. To over 6 feet.

Spawning: From October through winter in aquaria (unknown in wild). Mature at age 7.

Life Span: Unknown but may be long because of sedentary life and lack of predators.

Food: Fish and various hard-shelled invertebrates, such as crabs, sand dollars, sea urchins, and snails.

Habitat and Range: Older fish live in rocky coastal areas to at least 740 feet. Found from Southeast Alaska through Aleutian Islands. The Bering wolffish is found north of the Alaska Peninsula; the wolf-eel is more common in the south.

81

WATCHING ALASKA'S FISH

The easiest fish to watch in Alaska are spawning salmon. They can be found in numerous roadside streams from July through September and sometimes into December, depending on species and location. Watching species other than salmon, with a couple of exceptions, requires scuba gear and a wet or dry suit. Those who dive in Alaska's waters are usually rewarded with crystal-clear conditions (except during summer plankton blooms), brilliant colors, and sometimes a meal of abalone or Dungeness or king crab.

Animals also watch spawning salmon, and you can observe them, too. Black and brown bears love to eat salmon, and the methods they use to catch them are often comical. Although bears feed on spawning salmon in thousands of streams throughout Alaska, there are only a few areas where you can easily observe them because they are very wary of humans. Below, I list the areas where people can watch fish; I have noted the areas where bears are more accustomed to humans.

The various ways that gulls obtain salmon eggs from and near spawning salmon are also fun to watch. The small Bonaparte's gull hovers over the stream and plunges tern-like after drifting eggs. Mew gulls may work the quieter water areas by rapidly moving their feet up and down to create a sort of upwelling current that brings eggs to the surface. The large glaucous-winged gull may wade in among spawning salmon and induce a female to extrude eggs by punching her belly with its beak, then quickly move to the salmon's vent to catch and eat them. Gulls are present along most coastal streams wherever salmon spawn.

The young of many fish can also be observed in streams. The easiest to observe are Dolly Varden and coho salmon, but others, such as arctic grayling and chinook salmon young, can be found in several areas of Alaska. Dolly Varden and coho young spend from 1 to 4 years in streams before migrating to sea as smolts. During this rearing period they are very territorial and, if you are still, you can observe their behavior.

It helps to watch fish if you have Polaroid glasses, a comfortable place to sit, and patience. As you approach a stream, fish often scatter, but if you sit still for a while they usually return to normal behavior. For young fish, returning to normal behavior may take up to 15 minutes.

The list below includes established or well-known fish-watching sites. These have become more popular in recent years and new ones are being developed and designated. A number of these sites were developed by the U.S. Forest Service in cooperation with other agencies and private companies. Wildlife Viewing Area information sheets, which have maps and details about individual species, are available from the Forest Service's district and area offices. Another useful source is the Alaska Department of Fish and Game's *Alaska Wildlife Viewing Guide*.

If you're traveling along Alaska's highways, check *The MILEPOST* for the little fish symbols next to some entries—a number of these sites may be good places to look for fish.

◀ *Watching chum salmon spawn at Sheep Creek near Juneau.*

SOUTHEAST ALASKA

ADMIRALTY ISLAND: Stan Price Pack Creek Bear Viewing Facility, via floatplane or boat from Juneau. Obtain permit from U.S. Forest Service in Juneau.

GLACIER BAY NATIONAL PARK: Bartlett River; salmon (late summer).

HAINES: Chilkat Bald Eagle Preserve, 9.2 miles from Haines; excellent area to see bald eagles feeding on chum salmon (October, November).

HOONAH: Suntaheen Creek Fishpass. Take Forest Service Roads 8502 and 8530. Chum, pink (July, August), coho (late September, October).

HYDER: Fish Creek; chum and pink salmon, black and brown bears (July, August, September).

JUNEAU: Gastineau salmon hatchery, 3 miles north of Juneau; viewing window where chinook, chum, coho, and pink salmon and occasional Dolly Varden swim by.

- Salmon Creek and bake, 3 miles north of Juneau. Eat barbecued salmon and watch chum spawn (July, August).
- Sheep Creek, mile 3 Thane Road; chum (July, August, September).
- Steep Creek Fish Viewing, Mendenhall Glacier Visitors Center; sockeye (mid-June through mid-September), coho (mid- to late September through October), Dolly Varden (October, November).

KETCHIKAN: Ketchikan Creek runs right through town; good views of spawning salmon from Creek Street.

- Lunch Creek in Settler's Cove State Park, 17 miles north of Ketchikan; coho (August, September).
- Ward Lake, 6 miles north of Ketchikan via Tongass Highway and Ward Lake Road. Look for salmon from nature trail at lake outlet.

PETERSBURG: Blind Slough Rapids (mile 14.2 Mitkof Highway) and Crystal Lake Fish Hatchery (mile 17.2); salmon in summer and fall.

PRINCE OF WALES ISLAND: Cable Creek Fishpass. From Hollis follow road signs to Hydaburg, turn left after about 11 miles, and continue 8 miles. Coho and black bear (July, August, September).

- Dog Salmon Fishpass, via highway from ferry terminal in Hollis (10 miles), Hydaburg Road (8.8 miles), and Polk or

Alaska's Biogeographic Regions

RUSSIA
CHUKCHI SEA
ARCTIC OCEAN
Point Hope
Bering Strait
Wulik River
ARCTIC
Seward Peninsula
Kotzebue
BROOKS
Saint Lawrence Island
Nome
Norton Sound
Kobuk River
Selawik River
Colville River
BEAUFORT SEA
RANGE
G SEA
ALASKA
Yukon River
ARCTIC CIRCLE
Yukon River
KWIM
WESTERN
Kuskokwim River
Sleetmute
INTERIOR
Fairbanks
Yukon River
Wood River Lakes
Susitna River
Tanana River
Delta Junction
ISTOL BAY
Lake Iliamna
laska
Peninsula
Katmai Nat'l Park
Cook Inlet
Palmer
Anchorage
Copper River
U.S.A. CANADA
OUTHWESTERN
Homer
SOUTHCENTRAL
YUKON TERRITORY
Kodiak Island
Kenai Peninsula
Cordova
Prince William Sound
GULF OF ALASKA
Yakutat
Alsek River
Chilkat River
Haines
GLACIER BAY
Juneau
Taku River
BRITISH COLUMBIA
Hoonah
Sitka
Admiralty Island
Stikine River
PACIFIC OCEAN
Frederick Sound
Baranof Island
SOUTHEAST
Petersburg
Wrangell
Prince of Wales Island
Ketchikan
Dixon Entrance

N
E

0 miles 100
0 km 100

SOUTHWESTERN
Aleutian Islands
Alaska Peninsula
PACIFIC OCEAN

#21 Road (16.7 miles). Steelhead (February through May), sockeye (mid- to late July), pink, chum (August, September), coho (August through October).
- Rio Roberts Fish Viewing Platform at Rio Roberts Creek bridge, 14 miles west of Thorne Bay; coho (late August to October).

SITKA: Beaver Lake Grayling Viewing Area at Sawmill Creek campground; arctic grayling (mid-May to June).
- Indian River footbridge in Sitka National Historic Park; pink (late August through September).
- Starrigavan Creek at mile 7.6 Halibut Point Road; coho, pink (August, September).

WRANGELL: Anan Creek Wildlife Viewing Area, 30 miles southeast of Wrangell by boat or floatplane; pink salmon and black bear (late June to late August).

YAKUTAT: Nine Mile Bridge on Situk River, via Alsek Road; chinook, sockeye, pink, chum, coho, steelhead, Dolly Varden (April to November).
- Tawah Creek via Cannon Beach Road; sockeye, pink, coho (under Cannon Beach bridge between July and November).

SOUTHCENTRAL ALASKA

ANCHORAGE: Ship Creek Viewing Platform just east of Ocean Dock Road; chinook (early June to mid-July), coho, pink (mid-August to September).
- Campbell Creek; coho (August, September).
- Six Mile Creek at Elmendorf Air Force Base; sockeye, pink (August to mid-September).

CORDOVA: At mile 15 Copper River Highway; coho (September, October).

EAGLE RIVER: Chugach State Park visitors center, 12.7 miles from Eagle River on Eagle River Road; chinook (July), sockeye (August).

PALMER: Bodenburg Creek next to Old Glenn Highway, 5.3 miles from Palmer; sockeye, pink (late August through September).

SEWARD HIGHWAY: Potter Marsh Boardwalk, 9.6 miles from Anchorage; chinook (June), coho (August).
- Bird Creek, 24 miles from Anchorage; pink (July, August).
- Tern Lake outlet (Daves Creek) at junction of Seward and Sterling Highways, 37 miles from Seward; sockeye (months not given).

- Williwaw Fish Viewing Platform at Portage Valley, 45 miles from Anchorage; sockeye, chum (mid-August through October), coho (October).
- Moose Creek Fish Viewing Area, about 80 miles from Anchorage; sockeye (late July through August).

VALDEZ: Crooked Creek Information Site, mile 0.9 Richardson Highway; chum, pink (mid-June to late August).

INTERIOR ALASKA

DELTA JUNCTION: Delta River; chum (mid-October to late November).

- Delta Clearwater River off Jack Warren Road, 13 miles north of Delta; coho (mid-October to mid-November).

FAIRBANKS: Chena River, between miles 39 and 50, Chena Hot Springs Road; chinook, chum (mid-July to mid-August).

RICHARDSON HIGHWAY: Viewing area just downstream from Summit Lake outlet; sockeye (late July).

SOUTHWESTERN ALASKA

KATMAI NATIONAL PARK AND PRESERVE: Brooks River Falls, access via floatplane to Brooks Camp; contact National Park Service for permit; sockeye, brown bear (mid-July through September).

KODIAK ISLAND: Lake Rose Tead, on Pasagshak Bay Road, 8 miles from junction with Chiniak Road; spawning salmon (late summer, fall).

MCNEIL RIVER STATE GAME SANCTUARY: Fly from Homer, contact Alaska Department of Fish and Game for details on how to apply for one of the few visiting permits; salmon and brown bear (late summer).

WESTERN ALASKA

NOME: Road system crosses a number of streams where chinook, chum, pink, coho, Dolly Varden, and arctic grayling can be found.

ARCTIC ALASKA

DALTON HIGHWAY INCLUDING PART IN THE INTERIOR: Highway crosses a number of streams that contain arctic grayling; young most easily seen; adults spawn May and June; follow fish symbols in *The MILEPOST*.

SUGGESTED READING

Alaska Department of Fish and Game. 1989. Wildlife Notebook Series. Juneau.

Clemens, W. A., and G. V. Wilby. 1961. *Fishes of the Pacific Coast of Canada.* Fisheries Research Board of Canada. Bulletin 68, 2d ed.

Eschmeyer, W. N., and E. S. Herald. 1983. *A Field Guide to Pacific Coast Fishes.* The Peterson Field Guide Series. Boston: Houghton Mifflin Company.

Gotshall, D. W. 1989. *Pacific Coast Inshore Fishes.* 3d ed. (rev.). Monterey, Calif.: Sea Challengers.

Groot, C., and L. Margolis. 1991. *Pacific Salmon Life Histories.* Vancouver, B.C.: University of British Columbia Press.

Hart, J. L. 1973. *Pacific Fishes of Canada.* Bulletin of the Fisheries Research Board of Canada. Bulletin 180.

Idyll, C. P. 1964. *Abyss, The Deep Sea and the Creatures That Live in It.* New York: Thomas Y. Crowell Company.

Kramer, D. E., W. H. Barss, B. C. Paust, and B. E. Bracken. 1995. *Guide to Northeast Pacific Flatfishes.* Marine Advisory Bulletin 47.

Lamb, A., and P. Edgell. 1986. *Coastal Fishes of the Pacific Northwest.* Madiera Park, B.C.: Harbour Publishing.

Love, R. M. 1991. *Probably More Than You Want to Know About the Fishes of the Pacific Coast.* Santa Barbara, Calif.: Really Big Press.

McPhail, J. D., and C. C. Lindsey. 1970. *Freshwater Fishes of Northwestern Canada and Alaska.* Fisheries Research Board of Canada. Bulletin 173.

Morrow, J. E. 1980. *The Freshwater Fishes of Alaska.* Anchorage: Alaska Northwest Publishing Company.

O'Clair, R. M., R. H. Armstrong, and R. Carstensen. 1992. *The Nature of Southeast Alaska: A Guide to Plants, Animals and Habitats.* Seattle: Alaska Northwest Books.

Page, L. M., and B. M. Burr. 1991. *A Field Guide to Freshwater Fishes.* Peterson Field Guide Series. Boston: Houghton Mifflin Company.

Paxton, J. R. and W. N. Eschmeyer, eds. 1994. *Encyclopedia of Fishes.* San Diego, Calif: Academic Press.

Quast, J. C., and E. L. Hall. 1972. *List of Fishes of Alaska and Adjacent Waters with a Guide to Some of Their Literature.* Washington, D.C.: U.S. Dept. of Commerce, NOAA Technical Report NMFS SSRF-658.

Robins, C. R., et al. (eds). 1991. *Common and Scientific Names of Fishes from the United States and Canada.* Special Publication 20, 5th ed. Bethesda, Md.: American Fisheries Society.

Steelquist, R. 1992. *Field Guide to the Pacific Salmon.* Seattle: Sasquatch Books.

Stolz, J., and J. Schnell, eds. 1991. *Trout.* The Wildlife Series. Harrisburg, Pa.: Stackpole Books.

The MILEPOST. 1995-96. Bellevue, Wash.: Vernon Publications.

GLOSSARY

Amphipods Animals of the order Amphipoda. Laterally compressed crustaceans that often lie on their flattened sides. An important source of food for salmon young in estuaries.

Anadromous A fish that spends most of its life at sea but returns to fresh water to spawn. This classic definition applies only generally to Alaska's anadromous fish. Many—coho salmon, Dolly Varden, cutthroat trout, and steelhead—spend more time in fresh water than at sea. Because of Alaska's cold waters and short growing season, they need more time to reach a size at which they can tolerate seawater (*see also* Smolt). Also, many younger sea-run cutthroat and most younger sea-run Dolly Varden return to fresh water from the sea and do not spawn.

Arrow worms Tiny marine animals with torpedo-shaped bodies that can dart rapidly for short distances. Most species live their entire lives as plankton.

Barbel A whisker-like fleshy projection found in front of the mouth in some fish (especially cod).

Char Common name for members of the genus *Salvelinus*, which includes arctic char, brook trout, Dolly Varden, and lake trout. Many contemporary biologists use the spelling charr and the names brook charr and lake charr, instead of trout.

Cirrus (pl. cirri) A fleshy appendage resembling a small, thin flap of skin.

Clasping organs Fleshy modifications of the pelvic fins found in male cartilaginous fish, such as sharks, skates, and ratfish. They are used to transfer sperm to the female.

Compressed Flattened from side to side.

Continental shelf Part of the continent that is submerged in relatively shallow sea. Many of Alaska's groundfish are taken commercially along this shelf.

Copepods A class of crustaceans that are mostly minute inhabitants of the sea and fresh waters. Copepods are a major food of many fish and one of the most abundant animals in the world.

Crustacea A phylum of animals that includes crabs and shrimps and myriad smaller relatives that make up a major component of zooplankton.

Despot Refers to the dominant fish among a group of territorial fish. Most common among stream-dwelling Dolly Varden, arctic grayling, coho salmon young, and cutthroat and rainbow trout. The despot often claims the territory with the most food, such as at the head of a pool.

Euphausiids Shrimp-like crustaceans that often occur in enormous numbers as "krill." They provide food for many fish and the plankton-eating humpback whale.

Fecundity The number of eggs that a female fish is capable of releasing.

Fin rays and spines The narrow structures in a fish's fin that support it; they are usually connected to each other by a membrane. Rays are flexible and segmented; spines are hard and unsegmented. The number of rays and spines within a fin can be useful for identification, such as distinguishing salmon from trout and char.

Food chain Most aquatic organisms are linked to each other by what they eat—phytoplankton are eaten by zooplankton, which are eaten by fish such as Pacific sand lance and Pacific herring, which are eaten by larger fish such as cod and salmon, which are in turn eaten by other fish, mammals, and birds. The food chain makes a full circle because the carcasses of dead fish contribute essential nutrients for phytoplankton.

Fry A term used to describe many fish in their first year of life, especially salmon.

Gastropods A group of mollusks that includes slugs, snails, and whelks. Small freshwater snails are important in the diet of some fish, such as Dolly Varden, while they reside in lakes.

Gill arch The support to which gill filaments and gill rakers are attached.

Gill rakers Projections on the front edge of a fish's gill arch used to strain food from the water. The number of gill rakers may vary among species and can be used for identification; for example, to distinguish Dolly Varden from arctic char and chum salmon from sockeye.

Groundfish A term used to describe commercially caught marine fish that mostly dwell on or near the bottom. Includes walleye pollock, Pacific cod, sablefish, Atka mackerel, rockfish, and flatfish.

Introduced fish Generally refers to fish that have been introduced by humans in areas where they do not normally occur. In Alaska, brook trout are the only introduced nonnative species. A couple of species, such as American shad and Atlantic salmon, have made it into Alaska's waters on their own, after being released or escaping elsewhere. In Alaska, it is illegal to possess, transport, and release live fish or live fish eggs without a permit. On occasion, some species, such as Alaska blackfish and northern pike, have been illegally introduced into waters by the general public.

Larva A stage of development that fish and many invertebrates go through immediately after hatching. Most larvae are helpless, do not resemble adults, and have special requirements for survival. Fish larvae usually have a yolk sac attached from which they derive food.

Lateral line A line of pores that runs down the body of a fish from head to tail. These pores are connected to a canal just below the surface of the skin that is further connected via nerves to the fish's brain. The lateral line is very sensitive to currents and movement. This helps fish maintain tight schools, move in murky water, and sense the best current to swim in.

Mollusks A phylum of animals that includes clams, snails, and octopus. Most mollusk species have a hard calcareous shell as adults, but many mollusks living in the ocean have a free-floating (pelagic) larval stage. These larvae are a major part of the zooplankton and are an important source of food for plankton-eating fish.

Mysids An order of crustaceans that often form large swarms in estuaries where they constitute a major food of many fish.

Nemerteans Mostly marine ribbon worms that live as adults in sand and mud or in cracks and crevices in rocks. Their larvae contribute to the ocean's zooplankton.

Ostracods A class of small bivalve crustaceans that live in both fresh and salt waters. Some species occur in the plankton, but most are bottom dwellers.

Parr marks   Dark marks on the side of young salmon (except pink salmon), Dolly Varden, arctic char, trout, and round and pygmy whitefish. The shape, number, and location of parr marks can be useful in identifying the young of these fish.

Pheromones   Hormonal substances secreted by fish that can be detected in extremely minute amounts by other fish, especially the same species. Pheromones may be useful in locating home streams and specific spawning sites by anadromous fish.

Pelagic   Usually pertains to organisms, and their life styles, that frequent the water column, as opposed to those that live on or near the bottom substrate.

Pelvic axillary process   A narrow fleshy flap that projects to the rear of a fish just above each pelvic fin. All members of the family Salmonidae (salmon, trout, char, whitefish, and grayling) have one.

Plankton   Organisms that swim very feebly or not at all. Plankters drift about in the water currents. They include plants (phytoplankton) and animals (zooplankton). In Alaska's lakes most of the phytoplankton consists of microscopic algae—desmids, diatoms, and dinoflagellates; the zooplankton that fish eat consists mostly of crustacea—copepods and cladocerans. In contrast, the plankton in Alaska's salt waters is extremely diverse and comes from a variety of sources, including the free-swimming larvae of sponges, worms, mollusks, starfish, crabs, barnacles, and numerous other animals that live on the ocean floor as adults. Eggs and larvae of fish also contribute to the plankton. Some, such as cods and flounders, produce over 1 million eggs and young per fish.

Pyloric caeca   Fleshy tubes, like a bunch of worms, that attach at the junction of a fish's stomach and intestine.

Resident fish   Those fish that live their entire life in fresh water, as opposed to anadromous fish.

Roe   Usually refers to the mass of eggs within the ovarian membrane of a female fish, but also can refer to the milt or sperm of the male fish.

Sea-run   Usually refers to the anadromous form of fish that typically have both freshwater resident and anadromous populations, such as cutthroat trout and Dolly Varden.

Semelparous   Fish that die after spawning once. All salmon in Alaska are semelparous. Although trout and char can survive after spawning, many die, especially males that fight and injure themselves during courtship.

Smolt   A stage in the life of an anadromous fish when it first migrates to sea and has developed the physiological and behavioral processes to tolerate seawater. Smolts have an overall silvery appearance.

Swim bladder   (also called air and gas bladder)   A narrow, balloon-like organ that lies at the top of the body cavity. A fish can change the volume of air in its bladder so it can float at different depths without effort. Some fish do not have a swim bladder, especially those that spend most of their time on the bottom, such as sculpins and flounders.

Weir   A device used by biologists and early Natives to herd and trap fish migrating upstream.

Yolk-sac fry   Fish fry with their yolk-sac attached. Commonly used to describe salmon young after hatching and before emergence from the gravel, a period when they obtain nourishment from their yolk-sac.

INDEX

*Numbers in **boldface** refer to photographs.*

Alaska Northwest Books™ is proud to publish another
book in its Alaska Pocket Guide series, designed with the
curious traveler in mind. Ask for more books in this series at your
favorite bookstore, or contact Alaska Northwest Books™.

ALASKA NORTHWEST BOOKS™
An imprint of Graphic Arts Center Publishing Company
P.O. Box 10306, Portland, OR 97210
800-452-3032